The Ultimate Advantage: Your Guide to Winning in Commercial Insurance

By: Mitchell Brown

The Ultimate Advantage

The Ultimate Advantage

Table of Contents

Introduction 5

Chapter 1 9

Chapter 2 18

Chapter 3 26

Chapter 4 47

Chapter 5 59

Chapter 6 66

Chapter 7 77

Chapter 8 84

Chapter 9 101

Chapter 10 130

Chapter 11 135

Chapter 12 148

Chapter 13 155

Chapter 14 163

Chapter 15 180

Chapter 16 199

The Story of John 206

The Ultimate Advantage

Introduction: Claiming Your Ultimate Advantage

In the bustling world of insurance sales, standing out from the crowd is more than just an ambition—it's a necessity. As the landscape of commercial insurance continues to evolve, so does the craft of selling it. But amid the intricate policies and fluctuating market rates lies a pathway to unparalleled success. I've laid out this path for you in *The Ultimate Advantage*.

This book isn't just another manual—it's rooted in proven techniques, it serves as a comprehensive training guide that agencies can employ to sculpt elite sales professionals. And the outcomes? Accelerated sales, heightened agency value, and a significant reduction in producer validation time. Quite simply, the results you've been striving for.
In the ever-competitive world of commercial insurance sales, the difference between mediocrity and excellence often hinges on possessing the right set of tools and strategies. *The Ultimate Advantage* is more than just a guide; it's a compendium of battle-tested techniques and insights that give sales professionals an edge, setting them apart in an ocean of agents. Every chapter, every lesson enclosed within these pages, is a testament to the transformative power of knowledge. Armed with this playbook, agents don't just thrive—they dominate.

For rookies stepping into the vast realm of insurance sales, the challenges can seem insurmountable. Yet, even the most accomplished of veterans occasionally find themselves in need of a fresh perspective or a revitalized approach. This book offers solace to both. With its comprehensive exploration of the sales journey, it illuminates pathways for beginners and provides renewed vigor to those who have long treaded these waters, ensuring that every reader finds value tailored to their unique journey.

The Ultimate Advantage

In essence, this book is a clarion call to all who aspire to mastery in commercial insurance sales. It beckons agents to rise above the average, to seek out and seize every opportunity for growth, and to do so with both honor and ambition. Let *The Ultimate Advantage* be your trusted ally in this quest, guiding you towards unparalleled success in your career.

A venture like this isn't forged in isolation. I owe a vast chunk of my insights and successes to some of the most brilliant minds I've had the privilege to cross paths with. To my friends and mentors, Richard "Gordy" Bunch, Kyle Dean, Stephen Smith, Gene Darnell, Gary Jensen, Alicia Calhoun, Katie Sharkey, Tom Snyder, Judy Rush, Tom Francis, Tony Caldwell, Matt Masiello, Holly Herron, and Bill Dine—your guidance throughout the years has been the compass guiding me through uncharted waters.

Further gratitude goes out to the numerous salespeople, business leaders, account managers, underwriters, and risk managers who have enriched my journey. Every interaction, every shared story, every piece of advice has contributed to the blueprint laid out in these pages.

Moreover, my fifteen-year-long service alongside the valiant Soldiers, Sailors, Airmen, and Marines has been instrumental in shaping my perspectives and values. Their relentless drive, unwavering commitment, and unparalleled camaraderie have imbued in me lessons that extend far beyond the battlegrounds.

In the end, the essence of our pursuits, whether in insurance, leadership, or life itself, is captured aptly by a quote that has resonated with me profoundly: "Deeds not

Words"." It is not merely about what we say but what we do, how we act, and the tangible impact we make.

This book offers readers a unique blend of theoretical principles and a compelling narrative. Structurally, the book is designed in such a way that readers can dive into the theoretical foundations first, delving deep into the principles that underpin the world of commercial insurance sales. These initial chapters are meticulously crafted to offer a comprehensive understanding of the core concepts. Following this enlightening journey, the narrative shifts to the gripping fictional tale of John that portrays the growth and myriad challenges faced by a nascent producer. John's tale is more than just a story; it's an illustrative guide showcasing the application of the principles covered in the earlier sections.

Alternatively, for those who prefer a narrative-driven approach, they can plunge right into John's story, absorbing the intricacies of his journey as a new producer. This engrossing tale not only provides entertainment but also embeds invaluable lessons within its storyline. Once immersed in John's world, readers can then circle back to the theoretical chapters, enriching their understanding of the narrative with foundational principles.

Regardless of the approach, the combination of enlightening principles and John's enthralling journey offers readers a holistic and engaging experience, illuminating the world of producers from both a theoretical and practical perspective.

Welcome to *The Ultimate Advantage*. Let's embark on this transformative journey together.

Chapter 1: Welcome to Commercial Insurance

The Ultimate Advantage

Welcome to the world of commercial insurance sales—a realm where the stakes are high, the challenges are varied, and the rewards are plentiful. As you embark on this journey, it's crucial to grasp the vital role commercial producers play and the dynamic landscape they operate in.

The Thrill and Responsibility of Commercial Insurance

Dive deep into the pulsating heart of global commerce, and you'll find commercial insurance at its core. This isn't just any industry; it's the silent guardian and the quiet facilitator of dreams, ambitions, and economic ventures. Every skyscraper, every startup, every global conglomerate relies on the foundational principle of risk transfer, and as a commercial insurance salesperson, you are at the epicenter of it all.

Each day in this field is a testament to the vastness of human endeavor. As you collaborate with diverse businesses, from innovative tech startups to generations-old family-run establishments, you're not just selling a policy. You are granting them the confidence to innovate, expand, and reach for the stars, knowing they have a safety net as protection from potential setbacks.

But more than the transactions, it's the essence of being a part of a larger narrative that's truly exhilarating. When businesses thrive, economies grow. And behind every thriving business is a robust insurance policy, ensuring that the unforeseen hurdles do not derail dreams. That's the transfer of risk in action—an unsung hero that has quietly propelled our global economy forward for centuries.

So, as you navigate the exhilarating world of commercial insurance, remember: You are not just part of an industry; you are part of a legacy. A legacy that shoulders the aspirations of millions and stands as a cornerstone of our collective prosperity. Welcome to the high-stakes, high-reward universe of commercial insurance.

The Role and Significance of a Commercial Producer

At its core, a commercial producer's role is to safeguard the financial health of businesses. You are not merely selling a policy; you are offering peace of mind, ensuring that entrepreneurs can operate fearlessly, even in the face of unexpected challenges. Each policy is a promise—a vow that, come what may, their business's foundation remains secure.

But the role transcends beyond policy sales. Commercial producers often find themselves wearing multiple hats—risk assessor, business consultant, and trusted advisor. You get to delve deep into various industries, understanding their nuances, and tailoring solutions to fit. It's a continuous learning journey where every client brings a fresh set of challenges and opportunities.

The Dynamic Role of the Commercial Producer

In the vast realm of commerce, the commercial producer stands as a gatekeeper, an architect of stability, and a beacon of assurance. It's not just about policies; it's about promises and partnerships. Every handshake, every proposal, every conversation you have paves the way for business owners to achieve their dreams without the lurking shadows of unforeseen risks.

As a commercial producer, you are entrusted with the monumental task of ushering in opportunities that wouldn't traditionally cross the agency's threshold. It demands an intuition for markets, a nose for potential, and the acumen to recognize opportunities even before they fully form. You are not just a salesperson; you are the agency's forward scout, identifying and capturing potential in its nascent stage.

While the obvious goal is to protect businesses from risks, what is important is the trust businesses place in you. With every policy you offer, you're handing over a shield—a layer of protection that empowers businesses to forge ahead, even when the path seems treacherous.

But the journey of a commercial producer isn't linear. It requires the ability to adapt, to be fluid in your role. One day you're a risk assessor, analyzing potential vulnerabilities for a startup tech firm, and the next, you're a business consultant for a century-old manufacturing unit, offering insights to navigate modern challenges.

This role demands a comprehensive understanding, a holistic approach. You must immerse yourself in the intricate dance of global economies, regional trends, industry-specific challenges, and individual business goals. Every client, every industry brings with it a novel puzzle, and it's your expertise that pieces it together.

It isn't just about selling; it's about tailoring. The same policy doesn't fit all situations. As a trusted advisor, you're crafting bespoke solutions, designed with the precision of a jeweler ensuring that each facet aligns with the business's unique risk profile.

However, being a commercial producer also demands resilience. The market is ever evolving, and businesses' needs shift with it. Continuous learning, adaptation, and an insatiable curiosity are non-negotiable traits. The moment you stop learning is the moment you cease to be effective.

In essence, the role of a commercial producer is a mosaic of responsibilities and opportunities. It's a symphony of strategy, intuition, knowledge, and passion. With every client you assist, every policy you tailor, you're not just ensuring their present but safeguarding their future.

And as you stand at the intersection of ambition and assurance, remember: You're not merely a part of the commercial insurance world; you're shaping it, one policy, one promise, one business at a time.

Why Commercial Producers and Agencies Are Top Earners

The world of commercial insurance is vast, and the monetary rewards can be substantial. Several factors contribute to the impressive earning potential of commercial producers:

Diverse Industries and People:

Commercial insurance producers immerse themselves in a world filled with a vast range of businesses and sectors. Their daily engagements could span from advising a burgeoning tech startup on protecting their intellectual assets to strategizing with a large-scale manufacturer on safeguarding their intricate supply chains. This breadth of interactions offers producers an enriching experience, providing insights into various industries' intricacies and challenges. Building proficiency in additional industries not only enhances their knowledge base but also equips them to better understand the unique risk profiles associated with each one.

The beauty of this diversity is that it directly affects their product offerings. Every business, irrespective of its industry, requires specialized insurance products tailored to its particular risks. For producers, this means that their portfolio of insurance policies isn't merely vast, but also complex. Offering specialized policies for each sector means they are never restricted to the pricing models of any one kind of coverage. Instead, they have the flexibility to delve into multiple pricing structures, depending on the industry in question.

There's also an exciting challenge for producers here. Catering to such diverse sectors means they must constantly update and refine their knowledge. This perpetual learning curve ensures that their role remains dynamic, demanding a mix of research, networking, and hands-on experience. The broader the range of industries they cater to, the more avenues they open up for potential high-revenue commissions, thereby driving profitability.

Average Account Size:

At the heart of commercial insurance lies the sheer magnitude of operations it encompasses. Think of a sprawling corporate campus versus a single-family home. The corporate entity, due to its vast operations, inherently has numerous risk vectors. Bigger businesses with multifaceted operations face threats ranging from data breaches and lawsuits to operational disruptions. All these culminate in the necessity for extensive insurance coverage tailored to protect against a multitude of threats.

The ramifications of these complex risks are comprehensive insurance policies with high-limit coverage. These policies, in turn, command substantial premiums, reflecting the broad scope of protection they offer. This is where commercial insurance shines in terms of revenue. A single policy, tailored to safeguard a multinational conglomerate, can carry a premium that dwarfs numerous personal policies combined. For producers, this means that even one significant commercial account in their portfolio can be a game-changer in terms of revenue.

The Ultimate Advantage

This scale and scope of commercial insurance offer a promising avenue for agencies. It's a straightforward equation: bigger risks require more substantial coverage, which in turn means higher premiums. And with higher premiums come higher commissions. Therefore, agencies that pivot towards or specialize in commercial insurance often find themselves in an advantageous position in terms of revenue generation.

Value-Based Selling:

Commercial insurance is a domain where transactional relationships should be rare. Instead, every sale is rooted deeply in understanding, consultation, and tailored solutions. Businesses each come with their own set of unique challenges and vulnerabilities. Recognizing this, insurance producers must don a consultant's hat, delving deep into a company's operations, identifying potential pitfalls, and then crafting insurance solutions that resonate with those specific needs.

For clients, the real value lies not just in the policy but in the expertise that accompanies it. They aren't just looking for a piece of paper that promises compensation; they seek robust protection that aligns with their business's core values and operations. This shift from mere price-based selling to value-based selling means that producers are often pitching peace of mind and business continuity. They're offering a service that assures businesses that in the face of adversity, their operations will remain unhindered.

This value-driven approach to selling is what sets commercial insurance apart. Clients recognize and are willing to invest in a service that offers them tailored protection. They're more inclined to pay for a policy that's been crafted based on their unique challenges, rather than a generic, off-the-shelf solution. This willingness to invest in value ensures that commercial insurance producers are not just selling policies but are also cementing long-term, trust-based relationships with their clients.

Understanding the Commercial Insurance Landscape

To truly excel in the domain of commercial insurance, one needs more than a cursory understanding of various industries; one requires a deep grasp of the shifting sands of the commercial insurance landscape itself. This dynamic landscape, continuously morphing in response to technological developments, regulatory shifts, and world events, presents both challenges and opportunities for the astute producer.

The rise of cyber threats, for instance, has fundamentally transformed the risk profile of virtually every business, from tech startups storing sensitive user data to manufacturing giants reliant on integrated supply chains. Similarly, the broader geopolitical scenario, characterized by events such as global trade wars or pandemics, has tangible implications for businesses and, by extension, their insurance needs. As commercial insurance producers, one's role isn't just reactive; it's proactive. They aren't just responding to clients' needs but anticipating them, advising businesses on potential risks, and crafting policies that offer genuine protection.

A quintessential aspect of this landscape is the cyclical nature of the insurance market, oscillating between "hard" and "soft" phases. During a hard market, coverage may become more expensive and harder to come by. Underwriting standards tighten, policy wordings become more restrictive, and insurers become more selective about whom they'll cover. Conversely, a soft market is characterized by lower premiums, broader coverage, and more lenient underwriting criteria. Such fluctuations are influenced by a myriad of factors, from catastrophic global events and economic downturns to competition levels among insurers.

Further complicating the landscape is the mobility of carriers. It's not uncommon for insurance carriers to enter or exit specific states or lines of business, often in response to regulatory changes, market conditions, or past claims experiences in those sectors. For instance, if a particular line of business becomes too risky or unprofitable, a carrier might opt to pull out, leaving a gap in the market. Conversely, if they identify an underserved segment or one that aligns with their strategic direction, they might choose to enter, intensifying competition. This ebb and flow demand that producers remain vigilant, constantly updating their knowledge base, and forging strategic alliances.

The industries themselves are in a state of flux. Regulatory changes can redefine operational standards, technological innovations can disrupt traditional business models, and consumer preferences can shift market dynamics. A producer's proficiency is gauged not just by how they respond to these changes but by how well they anticipate them. For instance, a decade ago, the cannabis industry might have been on the fringes of the mainstream commercial realm. Today, with its growing legalization and acceptance, it presents a new frontier of risks and opportunities for insurers.

Thriving as a commercial insurance producer demands more than just an understanding of policies; it requires a holistic grasp of the broader ecosystem. It's about staying informed, anticipating market shifts, and being agile enough to pivot in response. The commercial insurance landscape, with all its complexities, beckons those ready to navigate its

The Ultimate Advantage

intricacies, always ensuring businesses are shielded from the unpredictable storms they might face.

Embracing a career as a commercial insurance producer is stepping into a world where each day is unique. It's about forging connections, understanding the intricacies of diverse industries, and providing solutions that truly matter. The journey might be challenging, but for those who are up for the task, the rewards—both monetary and in job satisfaction—are unparalleled.

Chapter 2: Foundations of Sales Psychology

The Importance of Sales Psychology in Commercial Insurance

In the intricate dance of sales, techniques and strategies often take center stage. However, before one can master these moves, there's a foundational element that needs understanding of the human psyche. Sales, at its core, is a deeply human endeavor, an intricate interplay of emotions, perceptions, and decisions. In commercial insurance, this becomes even more pronounced. Here, you're not just selling a policy; you're offering protection, peace of mind, and a safety net for businesses. To truly resonate with prospects, understanding their mindset, fears, aspirations, and motivations is not just beneficial; it's paramount.

Sales psychology, especially in the commercial insurance space, hinges on trust. Businesses are entrusting you with the protection of their livelihoods, their dreams, and the well-being of their stakeholders. Establishing this trust requires a profound understanding of their unique needs and the ability to empathize with their concerns. It's not just about rattling off policy details, but about showcasing genuine concern for their risks and offering tailored solutions.

Let's illustrate this with a story. David, a seasoned insurance producer, once encountered a tech startup founder, Sarah. Instead of diving straight into policy specifics, David began by asking about Sarah's journey, her aspirations for her company, and her biggest fears. Sarah shared her concerns about potential cyber threats, given the sensitive data they handled. David listened intently, recognizing not just the overt need for cyber liability insurance but also the underlying anxiety Sarah felt about her company's reputation and her customers' trust. He tailored his pitch to address these concerns, not just highlighting the coverage details, but also emphasizing how the policy would bolster her company's image and provide reassurance to her clientele. This personalized approach, rooted in understanding Sarah's motivations, sealed the deal.

In essence, leveraging sales psychology in commercial insurance is about going beyond the surface. It's about tapping into the deeper currents of emotion and perception, weaving these insights into your sales narrative, and forging genuine, trust-based connections. When producers move past mere transactions and step into the realm of relationship-building, they not only close deals but also cultivate lasting partnerships.

The Buyer's Journey: A Deep Dive

Understanding the buyer's journey is tantamount to unlocking the full potential of any sales strategy. Just like any traveler traversing an unknown path, potential clients navigate through distinct stages before arriving at a purchasing decision. By developing a deep understanding of each of these stages and tailoring strategies accordingly, insurance producers can guide prospects effectively, ensuring a smoother and more fruitful journey for both parties.

Awareness Stage:

Picture a business owner named Michael. He's recently realized that with the expansion of his manufacturing company, there seem to be new liabilities and risks he hasn't encountered before. He's vaguely aware of potential issues but can't precisely pinpoint them.

The Ultimate Advantage

Definition: This is the "Awareness Stage," where potential clients, much like Michael, recognize a problem but are still grappling to fully comprehend its nuances.

Role of the Producer: As a producer, this is the golden opportunity to position oneself as a beacon of knowledge. Imagine if Michael stumbled upon an insightful webinar or an article addressing common risks faced by expanding manufacturers; the focus of the webinar or article would not be directly selling any product because providing value and insights can be a game changer.

Methods: Offering webinars, crafting informative articles, curating e-books, or even providing general risk assessment tools can be invaluable. For instance, if Michael attended a webinar detailing the different challenges faced by growing manufacturers and found it helpful in his decision making, it would cement his view of the producer as a trusted resource.

Consideration Stage:

Fast forward a few weeks, and Michael, having garnered a clearer understanding of his challenges, is now actively seeking solutions. He's comparing different insurance policies, weighing out the pros and cons of each, and trying to figure out which one aligns with his company's needs.

Definition: Welcome to the "Consideration Stage." At this juncture, potential clients have a clear articulation of their problems and are on the lookout for viable solutions.

Role of the Producer: Producers need to step up and be the guiding light. Using the story of a similar manufacturing company, "Atlas Manufacturing," that faced and mitigated risks using a particular solution, can be illustrative. It's about showcasing how your offerings have been effective for others with similar challenges.

Methods: Employing case studies, solution comparison charts, and client testimonials can be crucial. If Michael came across a case study of "Atlas Manufacturing" detailing how they combated challenges using a specific insurance solution, it paints a relatable picture. Additionally, personalized risk assessments can further narrow down and tailor the solutions Michael might be considering.

Decision Stage:

A month into his search, armed with knowledge and options, Michael is on the brink of deciding. He's narrowed down his choices, assessed potential partners, and is almost ready to take the plunge.

Definition: This pivotal point is the "Decision Stage." Prospects, having sifted through solutions, are now primed to finalize their choice.

Role of the Producer: This is the producer's moment to shine. By emphasizing unique value propositions, showcasing unparalleled expertise, and elucidating the advantages of their offering, they can tilt the balance in their favor. Suppose a producer approached Michael with a comprehensive proposal, detailing not just the policy coverage but also the additional support, training, and resources their agency provides. This would underscore the value they bring to the table beyond just insurance.

Methods: Engaging in one-on-one consultations, presenting meticulously crafted proposals, and demonstrating the depth of support and resources an agency offers can make all the difference. For Michael, witnessing firsthand the dedication, expertise, and personalized attention he'd receive might just be the clincher.

The buyer's journey, though segmented into distinct stages, is a fluid continuum of discovery, understanding, and decision-making. By recognizing the unique needs, apprehensions, and aspirations prospects harbor at each stage, producers can craft bespoke strategies that resonate deeply. Whether it's the initial allure of knowledge, the comforting echo of a relatable story, or the decisive embrace of unparalleled value, mastering the art of guiding buyers through their journey is the linchpin of successful sales in commercial insurance.

Building Trust and Rapport: More than Just Selling Policies

In the world of commercial insurance, the true mettle of a producer isn't merely measured by the number of policies sold. It's gauged by the strength of the relationships forged. Let's delve deeper into the key pillars that underpin these relationships, illustrated by real-life stories.

Listening Actively:

Recall Sarah, the founder at a tech startup. When she met her first insurance agent, she was met with a barrage of policy details before she could even explain her unique business model. Frustrated, she sought another agent, David. Unlike the first agent, David began their interaction with a simple question: "Tell me about your vision for your company?" He listened intently, nodding, and taking notes. By the time Sarah was done, David not only understood her insurance needs but her aspirations and fears.

The lesson? Before offering solutions, ensure you fully grasp the client's needs and concerns. It's not just about hearing but understanding. *Listen more than you speak.*

Authenticity:

Jonathan, an experienced restaurant owner, met countless insurance agents over his career. But he often felt like just another sale on their charts. That was until he met Maya. Maya was different. Instead of launching into a rehearsed pitch, she shared her genuine excitement about a dish she tried at one of his establishments. Their interaction felt real, devoid of the usual salesy veneer.

Being genuine, showing real interest and emotion, makes a difference. Clients, like Jonathan, can discern when a producer is genuine versus when they're just looking to make a quick sale. *Authenticity breeds trust.*

Shared Stories:

Mike, an insurance producer, once sat across from a client who ran a family-owned brewery. As they discussed the business's history, Mike shared a personal story about his grandfather, who also ran a small brewery. He talked about the challenges his grandfather faced during a particularly bad winter storm and how proper insurance saved the business from potential ruin. This shared narrative not only humanized Mike but showcased his deep understanding of the industry.

Relating to your clients through relevant experiences demonstrates not just empathy but also expertise. It fosters a deeper connection, rooted in shared experiences and challenges overcome.

Consistent Follow-Up:

Three months after selling a comprehensive policy to Alice, a bookstore owner, agent Peter dropped by. Not for another sale or upsell, but to see how she was doing. He inquired about a recent store event Alice had mentioned in their previous meetings. These seemingly small gestures made Alice feel valued.

Regular check-ins, even without the immediate prospect of a sale, send a powerful message. They show clients, like Alice, that you value the relationship beyond just transactions. *Consistent follow-up solidifies trust.*

Transparency:

Henry, a tech startup founder, was once burned by hidden fees in an insurance policy. The experience made him wary. Enter Clara, a producer who made it her mission to be crystal clear. She painstakingly walked Henry through every clause, ensuring he understood costs, potential scenarios, and any caveats.

Being forthright about services, their costs, and all relevant details avoids future misunderstandings. For clients like Henry, this clarity isn't just appreciated; it's a prerequisite. *Transparency is the bedrock of trust.*

Trust isn't built overnight. It's a mosaic, crafted piece by piece, interaction by interaction. In the multifaceted world of commercial insurance, understanding the underlying psychology of sales and trust-building gives producers a distinct edge. By genuinely comprehending and empathizing with the buyer's journey and fostering

The Ultimate Advantage

authentic trust, producers can move beyond mere transactions. They can cultivate rich, meaningful, and enduring relationships with their clients.

In our next chapter, we'll delve deeper, exploring practical techniques and strategies, all grounded in this profound understanding of sales psychology. Our aim? Equipping you to not just approach and engage prospects but to transform them into staunch, loyal clients.

Chapter 3: Start Building a Book of Business.

Why Prospecting Is the Lifeblood of Commercial Insurance Sales

In the multifaceted world of commercial insurance sales, success often hinges on the agent's capacity to unearth and engage potential clients, commonly referred to as prospects. This isn't a simple numbers game. Successful prospecting revolves around pinpointing the right leads, the ones who not only need your service but value it. First we have to determine who are our ideal customers.

Building the Ideal Customer Profile

Developing ideal customer profiles is a crucial step for commercial insurance producers in targeting and serving their clients effectively. A valuable approach to this process is using the acronym SALT, which stands for Size, Activity, Location, and Timeframe. This method helps in categorizing and understanding potential clients more comprehensively, ensuring that the services offered align perfectly with their specific needs.

Size: The 'Size' aspect of SALT involves understanding the scale of a potential client's operations, which is a significant determinant of their insurance needs. Size can be gauged through various metrics such as the number of vehicles (if their business is transport or delivery-oriented), property values (important for real estate or businesses with significant physical assets), the number of employees (for liability and worker's compensation insurance) or estimated annual sales. Each of these factors drives the premium and shapes the type and extent of coverage required. For example, a business with a large fleet of vehicles will have different insurance needs compared to a software company with high annual sales but minimal physical assets.

Activity: 'Activity' refers to the nature of the business or what the company does. This can range from manufacturing, retail, technology services, to healthcare. Each industry and activity comes with its unique risks and challenges. Understanding the specific activities of a potential client helps in tailoring insurance solutions that cover industry-specific risks. For instance, a manufacturing company might need extensive property and liability insurance, while a healthcare provider would require substantial malpractice coverage.

Location: The 'Location' of a business significantly impacts its insurance needs. Factors such as local weather patterns, crime rates, and proximity to hazardous materials can influence the risk profile. For instance, a business located in an area prone to natural disasters like floods or earthquakes will have different insurance needs compared to one in a relatively stable area.

Timeframe: Finally, 'Timeframe' is crucial in understanding when a potential client's current insurance policies are due for renewal or when they need to make critical insurance decisions. This knowledge allows insurance producers to approach prospects at the most opportune time, providing them with timely and relevant insurance options. Understanding the timeframe helps in planning and aligning your approach to meet their needs effectively.

By considering these SALT factors, commercial insurance producers can build precise and actionable customer profiles, leading to more effective targeting, better customer relationships, and ultimately, a more successful insurance practice.

Let me give a real-world example of how this works. Robbie was a commercial producer who wanted to target gymnastic facilities and golf courses. Robbie's strategic use of the SALT acronym enabled him to define and refine his ideal customer profiles for specific industries, with remarkable precision. By breaking down the SALT acronym, we can understand how he tailored his approach for each industry.

Size: For gymnastics facilities, Robbie focused on medium-sized establishments. This size category likely reflects a balance between the number of participants and the scale of operations, which in turn affects the type and scope of insurance needed. A medium-sized facility would have substantial, but manageable, risks associated with both recreational and competitive gymnastics programs. In the case of golf courses, targeting mid-sized courses suggests he considered factors like the area of the property and the number of holes, both of which can influence insurance premiums and requirements.

Activity: Robbie's distinction in the gymnastics facilities' activities - offering both recreational and competitive programs - highlights his attention to the varied risks these two different programs might pose. Recreational activities might involve a broader, potentially less experienced audience, whereas competitive programs could entail higher risks due to the advanced nature of the activities. For golf courses, targeting those hosting occasional events implies a consideration for additional liabilities and insurance needs that arise during events compared to normal operations.

Location: By targeting gymnastics facilities in suburban areas and golf courses near urban areas, Robbie shows an understanding of how location influences risk. Suburban areas for gymnastics facilities might indicate a family-oriented clientele and potentially fewer risks compared to a densely populated urban location. For golf courses, being near urban areas could mean a higher volume of visitors and a different set of risks and exposure.

Timeframe: Robbie's focus on facilities with insurance policies renewing within specific timeframes (six months for gymnastics facilities, and for golf courses) demonstrates his strategic approach in timing his outreach. This ensures that he engages with potential clients when they are most likely considering their insurance options, thus increasing the chances of his services being relevant and timely.

Market Research:

To truly deliver what your potential clients need, a deep understanding of their industry is crucial. This is where market research plays a pivotal role. When you comprehend the intricacies and challenges of a particular sector, you can tailor your offerings and communicate them in a way that strikes a chord.

Leveraging Modern Tools

LinkedIn:
In today's digital age, LinkedIn stands as a powerful and indispensable tool for insurance agents looking to connect with commercial clients. This professional networking platform offers a unique and targeted approach to business development, far surpassing traditional methods. With LinkedIn, agents have access to a vast network of industry professionals and businesses across various sectors. This access not only allows for the identification of potential clients but also enables agents to engage with them directly

through informed and personalized outreach. The platform's advanced search capabilities and the ability to join industry-specific groups provide a wealth of opportunities for agents to position themselves as industry experts, share valuable content, and build credibility within their target markets. By leveraging LinkedIn, commercial producers can effectively network, understand client needs, and build relationships that lead to successful commercial client acquisition in the modern business landscape.

- **Advanced Search:** LinkedIn's advanced search is a game-changer. It allows producers to target decision-makers within specific industries or regions, enhancing the precision of outreach efforts.

- **Content Sharing:** Being an active voice in your field can amplify your presence. By sharing insightful content on commercial insurance, you position yourself as an industry expert, which can draw potential clients towards you.

Greg was a commercial insurance producer who had always believed in the power of networking, but it was only when he began to fully utilize LinkedIn that he unlocked a new level of success. Recognizing the platform as a goldmine for targeted prospecting, Greg set out on a mission to use LinkedIn to its fullest extent.

Leveraging LinkedIn Search

The first thing Greg did was to hone his LinkedIn search skills. He was targeting small to medium-sized tech companies and manufacturing businesses. Using the advanced search feature, he applied multiple filters to find decision-makers in these sectors. One filter he found particularly useful was sorting by educational background. Having graduated from State University, Greg looked for professionals who had also attended the same school, creating a common point of interest right from the get-go.

Establishing Common Ground

It's amazing how much a shared alma mater can break the ice. Greg crafted personalized connection requests, mentioning their shared educational background and expressing a desire to discuss how he could provide value for their company's insurance needs. The response rate was impressive. People who otherwise might have ignored the request found the commonality intriguing enough to engage.

Posting Educational Content

To further solidify his presence as an industry thought leader, Greg started posting educational blog posts on LinkedIn. He focused on topics relevant to the industries he was targeting. One week he posted about "Cyber Risks for Tech Companies in the Digital Age," and the next he discussed "Safety Liabilities in Manufacturing: What Business Owners Need to Know." These posts were not just about random topics; they were carefully chosen to address the pain points he had identified during his LinkedIn searches and subsequent conversations.

Generating Leads through Content

The strategy of posting insightful blog posts paid off handsomely. Not only did these articles get shared within LinkedIn groups dedicated to tech and manufacturing, but they also started conversations with key decision-makers. Each blog post had a call to action at the end, inviting the reader to reach out to Greg for a personalized consultation, and many did.

Cultivating Relationships

The Ultimate Advantage

Armed with an array of new connections and inquiries, Greg was careful not to rush the sales process. He followed up on each engagement with a thank-you message and an offer to discuss their specific insurance needs further. His posts continued to provide value, keeping him at the forefront of their minds, even if they weren't immediately ready to decide.

By mastering the LinkedIn platform, particularly its advanced search features and content-sharing capabilities, Greg not only found a goldmine of qualified prospects but also positioned himself as an industry expert. The educational content acted as a soft selling tool, warming up leads before Greg even had to make the first pitch. Plus, the shared educational background provided a natural conversation starter, reducing the coldness of the outreach.

The power of LinkedIn for Greg wasn't just in its ability to find leads; it was also in the platform's capacity to facilitate meaningful relationships built on mutual interests and industry-specific challenges. This comprehensive approach transformed Greg from just another salesperson into a trusted resource, setting the stage for long-term client relationships that went beyond transactional interactions.

As a result of his LinkedIn strategy, Greg saw a substantial increase in his client acquisition rate, he was able to target leads more efficiently and converted them more effectively. It was a win-win scenario where both Greg and his clients found value, proving that when used wisely, LinkedIn can be an extraordinary tool for success in the commercial insurance sector.

Industry Databases:

Subscribing to relevant databases can provide a wealth of information. These platforms can offer insights into a company's performance, its key decision-makers, and prevailing industry trends, equipping you with knowledge that can be invaluable during pitches.

Email Campaign Tools:

Utilizing platforms like Mailchimp or HubSpot helps segment and target audiences effectively. Sending tailored content, relevant to each segment's pain points, can significantly increase engagement and conversion rates.

Crafting an Effective Email Campaign

Setting Objectives

The first step in crafting an effective email campaign is to define your objectives clearly. Knowing whether you aim to build brand awareness, generate leads, or drive user engagement helps focus the campaign. The objectives should align with your broader business goals, and they will inform the key performance indicators (KPIs) you'll track.

Identifying Pain Points

Understanding your target audience's pain points is crucial for creating compelling content. Tailor your email messages to address specific challenges or needs that your prospects or clients may have. For instance, if you are targeting small businesses, you might discuss the issue of high insurance premiums or inadequate coverage. Addressing pain points not only establishes relevance but also builds trust.

Segmenting Your Audience

One of the major advantages of using email campaign platforms like HubSpot or Mailchimp is the ability to segment your audience. You can segment by industry, company size, or even specific behaviors exhibited by the users like clicking on a previous email. Segmenting ensures that your messages resonate more deeply because they can be customized to specific groups.

KPIs to Track

Establishing concrete Key Performance Indicators (KPIs) is a non-negotiable component for the success of your email campaign. It's not just about tracking metrics; it's about knowing precisely which metrics will give you a clear snapshot of your campaign's performance. The KPIs you absolutely must monitor are open rates, click-through rates, conversion rates, and most importantly, the Return on Investment (ROI) of the campaign. Don't just gloss over these metrics; scrutinize them. Each one serves as a crucial barometer for different facets of your campaign. Open rates tell you how compelling your subject line and timing are, click-through rates indicate the quality and relevance of your content, and conversion rates show you how effective your call to action is. ROI, the ultimate metric, validates the financial viability of your campaign. Keeping tabs on these KPIs isn't merely a best practice; it's essential for the tactical evolution of your email marketing *strategy.*

Automating the Campaign

Both HubSpot and Mailchimp offer robust automation features. From sending welcome emails to new subscribers to triggering emails based on user behavior, automation can significantly improve efficiency. Automation also allows for more personalized interactions with your audience, as you can set triggers based on specific actions or time frames, ensuring that you're reaching out when your product or service is most relevant to them.

Crafting Engaging Content

No campaign will succeed without compelling content. Aim for a balanced mix of informative and promotional content. Use the subject line to capture their attention and get your email opened. The body should deliver on any promises made in the subject line and conclude with a clear call-to-action that guides the reader in what to do next.

Creating Raving Fans

Delivering consistently high-value content will not only help you achieve your immediate campaign objectives but will also turn your audience into fans who look forward to your emails. This not only increases your open rates but also fosters brand loyalty. Listen to your audience's feedback and be prepared to make real-time adjustments to your campaign to better serve their needs.

Analyzing and Tweaking

Finally, after your campaign has run its course, take time to analyze the results. Look at your KPIs, see what worked and what didn't, and take the time to understand why. Use these insights to tweak or overhaul your next campaign. The key to a successful email marketing strategy is iterative improvement, driven by robust analysis and a keen understanding of your audience's needs and behaviors.

Sample Email

Subject: Is Your Marina's Spill Prevention Plan Up-to-Date? Take Action Now!

Dear [Marina Owner's Name],

I hope this email finds you well. My name is [Your Name], and I'm with [Your Company], specialists in comprehensive insurance solutions for marinas like yours. One of the key challenges we've identified that marina owners often face is keeping up-to-date with Spill Prevention, Control, and Countermeasure (SPCC) Plans. Regulations around SPCC are continually evolving, and failure to keep up can not only put your marina at environmental risk but also result in heavy fines.

Is an Updated SPCC Plan Required for Your Size of Marina?

The first step to compliance is knowing whether your marina requires an updated SPCC Plan under the latest EPA guidelines. Generally, marinas with aboveground oil storage capacity greater than 1,320 gallons must have a plan in place. Failing to comply can lead to hefty penalties that can easily run into the tens of thousands.

Don't Risk It - Ensure Compliance

Keeping your SPCC Plan up-to-date can be a labor-intensive process, involving site inspections, employee training, and liaising with state and local authorities. Your time is precious, and that's why we offer a specialized insurance package that includes SPCC Plan assessment and updating.

Take Action Today

Given the importance of this matter, we would like to offer a complimentary SPCC Plan review for your marina. Our team of experts can identify any areas where you may not be in full compliance, thus mitigating potential risks and saving you from possible penalties. To schedule your free review, click here [insert link to scheduling page].

In closing, adherence to SPCC regulations is not just about avoiding fines; it's about being a responsible steward of our environment. We look forward to the opportunity to support your marina in fulfilling both its regulatory and environmental commitments.

Best regards, [Your Name] [Your Position] [Your Contact Information]

The Ultimate Advantage

> *P.S. Stay ahead of the curve by getting your SPCC Plan assessed by experts. Schedule your free review today! [insert link to scheduling page]*

Feel free to adjust this template to suit your specific needs and branding. The goal is to address the marina owners' immediate pain point—the need for an updated SPCC Plan—while also offering a concrete next step.

The sample email above targets marina owners and is designed to address a very specific and urgent pain point: the need for an updated Spill Prevention, Control, and Countermeasure (SPCC) Plan. In many industries, and particularly those involving environmental risks like marinas, regulatory compliance is not just a best practice—it's a necessity. Failing to comply can result in severe financial penalties, not to mention the risk to the environment. This serves as the immediate issue or "pain point" that the email focuses on.

The structure of the email is tailored to not only highlight this pressing issue but also to offer a solution. The email does this by mentioning the urgency and the regulatory requirements around the SPCC Plan and then offering the marina owner a free SPCC Plan review. This positions the sender not as a salesperson but as a problem solver. It's a value-first approach that can be very effective for building trust and getting the recipient to take the next step.

Lastly, the email includes a clear and compelling Call to Action (CTA) at the end, encouraging the marina owner to schedule their free SPCC Plan review. A good CTA is crucial for directing the recipient to take the next steps. It eliminates ambiguity and makes it easy for the recipient to act, which in turn, makes it more likely that they will.

In summary, this sample email for marinas is effective because it identifies a critical pain point, offers a valuable solution, and includes a clear call to action. It's designed to create urgency, offer value, and make it simple for the recipient to take the next step. This trifecta makes it much more likely that the email will achieve its desired outcome: engaging the marina owner and moving them closer to becoming a client.

Traditional Methods That Still Work

Referrals:

Getting referrals is a crucial part of sustaining and growing a business, yet it's often one of the most overlooked areas in sales strategy. A good referral not only brings in a new client but does so with a level of trust and credibility that is hard to gain through cold outreach. There are two main channels through which you can effectively get referrals: Centers of Influence (COIs) and your current client base. Here's how to tap into each.

For commercial insurance agents, the process of leveraging Centers of Influence (COIs) is pivotal to creating a robust network that delivers consistent and quality referrals. But, who are these COIs, and how does one go about fostering meaningful relationships with them?

Identifying COIs: Centers of Influence are not limited to just one or two professions. While accountants and lawyers remain the traditional go-to COIs, in today's dynamic market, the horizon has expanded. Fractional CFOs, who offer part-time financial leadership to businesses, have become significant influencers. These professionals typically engage with various firms, providing a goldmine of networking opportunities. Similarly, business attorneys, who advise businesses on their legal rights, responsibilities, and obligations, come into regular contact with firms that might need insurance products. Recognizing these unique roles and their potential in connecting you to your target market is the first step towards a successful COI strategy.

Initial Approach and Building a Relationship: The foundation of any strong business relationship is trust. Instead of rushing into seeking referrals, invest time in nurturing a bond with the COIs. A casual coffee or a business lunch can be a great way to initiate this. During these interactions, make genuine efforts to understand their industry, challenges, and clients. A two-way street, where you can also provide them with potential referrals or insights from your end can be exceptionally rewarding.

Articulate Your Value Proposition: It's not enough for COIs to know that you're an insurance agent; they need to understand your unique value. What differentiates you from other agents? What's your specialty? Maybe you offer tailored solutions for specific industries, or perhaps you're known for your exceptional customer service. Make it clear who you serve best and why you're the top choice for those clients.

Set up a Referral System: With the foundation laid and mutual understanding established, it's time to formalize the relationship. Discuss with your COIs the best way for them to introduce new prospects to you. While some may prefer a commission-based structure, others might be content with a mutual-referral arrangement. The key is to create a system that's transparent, ethical, and beneficial for all parties involved.

Follow-up and Acknowledgment: A referral is a testament to the trust your COIs place in you. It's essential to keep them in the loop about the business you receive through them. Regular updates not only foster transparency but also give them the confidence that their referrals are in good hands. And, of course, never underestimate the power of a simple "thank you." Gratitude can go a long way in strengthening and maintaining these crucial business relationships.

COIs like Fractional CFOs and business attorneys are invaluable assets. They can open doors to a plethora of potential clients. However, the key lies in building, nurturing, and maintaining these relationships with patience, understanding, and mutual respect.

Gaining Referrals from Current Clients

Timing Is Key: The best time to ask for a referral is right after a successful deliverable or positive review. The client is happy and more likely to advocate for you at this point.

Direct Approach: Sometimes, being direct and simply asking is the best approach. Of course, this has to be handled tactfully. You could say, "We're thrilled you're happy with our services. Do you know anyone else who might benefit from what we offer?"

Make It Easy for Them: Don't make your client to do the heavy lifting. Provide them with a template they can use to make the introduction. This makes it easier for them to advocate for you.

Incentivize: Some businesses offer discounts or small freebies as a thank-you for a referral. This creates a win-win scenario where the client feels appreciated for their effort.

Leverage Social Proof: Use testimonials or case studies to demonstrate your effectiveness. Sharing these with your current clients makes them more comfortable sending referrals to you.

Regular Follow-up: Just like with COIs, always acknowledge, and thank your clients for referrals. This can be as simple as a thank-you note or as substantial as a gift or discount on future services.

Building a Referral Culture

One way to ensure a steady flow of referrals is to make it part of your company culture. Train your team to spot opportunities for referrals, both with COIs and current clients. Create systems and processes that make it easy to handle referrals when they come in.

Track and Measure

Whatever methods you use, make sure to track the effectiveness of your referral efforts. This will help you understand what's working and where you need to make changes. Some useful Key Performance Indicators (KPIs) might include the number of referrals received, the conversion rate of referrals, and the lifetime value of clients acquired through referrals.

Getting referrals isn't just a one-time activity; it's an ongoing process that should be integrated into your overall business strategy. By building strong relationships with both Centers of Influence and your current client base, you can create a powerful referral network that fuels your business growth.

Cold Calling:

Although daunting for many, cold calling has its merits. When coupled with prior research and a well-crafted pitch, it's a technique that can yield positive results. Here, preparation is key.

Cold calling has been a long-standing practice in the sales industry, and even in the age of digital marketing, it still has its place, especially in complex fields like commercial insurance. While cold calling might seem archaic or invasive to some, when done correctly, it can be an effective way to reach potential clients, establish rapport, and most importantly, set up meetings to discuss individualized risk portfolios.

Cold calling, often viewed with trepidation, is an art form that, when mastered, can yield impressive results for commercial insurance agents.

Preparation is your foundation. Knowledge about the prospect and their industry primes you for success. In the world of commercial insurance, understanding specific risks, industry benchmarks, and prevailing trends can offer a persuasive advantage. When you call armed with insights, it demonstrates diligence and genuine interest, making the conversation more engaging and fruitful.

Targeting is about precision. The best outcomes arise when your prospect aligns with your ideal client profile. It saves both time and resources, allowing you to focus energy on potential leads that matter. Remember, it's less about the number of calls and more about the quality of the conversation.

Scripting offers guidance. While the conversation should flow organically, a script acts as a safety net. It ensures you convey key points and maintain a coherent narrative. However, sounding too rehearsed can deter prospects. Strive for a balance where you're equipped with a plan but can also improvise.

Timing can be a game-changer. Picture this: calling a potential client when they're least occupied increases your chances of engagement. The beginning and end of business hours are usually golden windows. However, it's always good to gauge and experiment to find what works best for your clientele.

Lastly, **Follow-up** is where consolidation happens. A cold call should not be an isolated event but the start of a budding relationship. Following up with an email or another call can keep the conversation going, potentially turning a cold lead into a warm prospect and eventually, a loyal client.

To sum up, cold calling, when approached strategically, becomes less daunting and more of a structured process that can be optimized over time. With preparation, targeting, scripting, timing, and diligent follow-up, commercial insurance agents can not only generate leads but also foster lasting relationships.

The Journey of a Young Producer

Meet Tom, a young commercial insurance producer eager to make his mark. On his first week, he decided to try cold calling without much training. Tom's initial approach was to read directly from a generic script, and he focused on trying to explain insurance policies on the call itself. As a result, most of his calls were met with instant rejections or led to long conversations that went nowhere.

The Ultimate Advantage

Feeling frustrated but determined to improve, Tom sought advice from Tina, a seasoned producer in his firm. She emphasized that the goal of a cold call for commercial insurance is not to close a sale but to secure a meeting where individual risks can be assessed and discussed. Tom took this to heart and adjusted his strategy. He started by conducting preliminary research on each company he was about to call, tailored his script to address industry-specific pain points, and aimed to set up in-person meetings to discuss individual risk profiles.

On implementing these changes, Tom noticed immediate results. Not only were prospects more receptive, but they were also more willing to set up meetings to explore tailored risk solutions. Within weeks, he had a pipeline of potential clients scheduled for discussions, thanks to the power of effective cold calling.

Tracking and Metrics

Cold calling is a numbers game, but it's also a strategy game. Track your calls, note the responses, and make necessary adjustments. Some KPIs to track might include:

- Number of calls made.

- Number of meetings set up.

- Conversion rate (from call to meeting)

- Quality of leads generated.

In commercial insurance, where understanding a client's unique set of risks is essential for offering the most suitable policy, cold calling serves as an initial point of contact that can lead to a meaningful dialogue. Effective cold calling is not just about the quantity but also the quality of conversations. It's about reaching the right people with the right message and setting the stage for a deeper, more valuable interaction down the line.

Cold Call Script for the Logging Industry

(Note: The goal of this call is to secure a meeting to discuss the potential client's individual risks and needs, not to close a sale over the phone.)

Producer: "Hello, is this [Prospect's Name]?"

Prospect: "Yes, this is [Prospect's Name]. Who is this?"

Producer: "Hi [Prospect's Name], this is [Your Name] from [Your Company]. I hope I'm catching you at a good time. I noticed that [Prospect's Company Name] has been making significant strides in the logging industry, and I wanted to congratulate you on that. Your industry faces a unique set of risks and challenges that we specialize in helping with. Do you have a few minutes to talk?"

(Note: It's crucial to mention something specific about their business or industry here to show you've done your homework.)

Prospect: "I'm a little busy, but what is this about?"

Producer: "I understand you're busy, and I'll be brief. We've been working with companies in the logging industry to significantly improve their risk profiles, thereby cutting down their total cost of risk and improving safety measures. Could we schedule a meeting this week to discuss how we might be able to assist [Prospect's Company Name] in a similar manner?"

Prospect: "Hmm, I might be interested. What would be the next steps?"

Producer: "Great to hear. The next step would be a brief meeting to discuss the specific challenges and needs of [Prospect's Company Name]. I can bring along some case studies that show how we've helped similar companies in the logging industry along with some bench marking data to show where the markets are and where they are heading. Would you be available for a thirty-minute meeting this week?"

Prospect: "Alright, let's schedule a meeting."

Producer: "Fantastic! I'll send over a calendar invite and some preliminary information we can discuss. Thank you for your time, [Prospect's Name], and I'm looking forward to our meeting."

Prospect: "Me too. Goodbye."

Producer: "Goodbye, [Prospect's Name]. Have a great day!"

The key to this script's effectiveness lies in its specificity to the logging industry, as well as its focus on scheduling a meeting rather than pushing for an immediate sale. You'll notice that the script is geared towards identifying the prospect's pain points and offering a targeted solution, which is the ideal way to approach cold calling in specialized industries like logging.

The world of commercial insurance is vast, and the potential for growth is immense. The key lies in effective prospecting—understanding your audience, leveraging the right tools, and nurturing genuine relationships. As we progress, we'll delve deeper into the nuances of converting these prospects into loyal clients.

Chapter 4: The Consultative Sales Approach

Transforming Sales through Deep Understanding and Partnership

The consultative sales approach is more than just a sales tactic; it's a philosophy that places the customer's needs at the forefront of the interaction. Instead of pushing a product or service, the consultative salesperson becomes an expert advisor, tailoring solutions to solve a customer's specific challenges or pain points. This creates a win-win scenario where the customer feels understood and valued, and the salesperson is more likely to close a deal that results in a long-term relationship.

One of the primary advantages of the consultative sales approach is that it shifts the focus of the interaction from the price to the value being delivered. This is crucial in industries like commercial insurance where the lowest price doesn't always equal the best coverage or the most appropriate risk management strategies. Instead of the buyer's primary focus being comparison shopping based on pricing, the goal becomes finding an agent who can best help them understand and manage their unique set of risks.

This brings us to the concept of Total Cost of Risk (TCOR). Unlike simple premium costs, TCOR considers various other costs related to risk, including retained losses, loss control measures, and administrative costs. Discussing TCOR rather than just the insurance premium price opens up a more comprehensive dialogue about the customer's overall business health and risk management strategy. It provides a more accurate picture of what they're actually spending and where there might be opportunities for improvements or cost savings.

Total Cost of Risk (TCOR) is a comprehensive financial metric used to identify and quantify all the costs associated with a company's risk management efforts. Contrary to popular belief, TCOR goes beyond just insurance premiums. It encapsulates a variety of factors, including self-insured losses, administrative costs, and risk control expenses. Essentially, TCOR provides a more nuanced and accurate picture of how much a business is truly spending to identify, manage, and mitigate risks.

For example, while an insurance premium might cover potential future liabilities, what about the expenses associated with filing claims, or the internal labor needed to manage safety and compliance programs? There might also be hidden or indirect costs, such as the loss of productivity following an accident or incident. TCOR takes all these elements into account, offering a holistic approach to understanding the financial implications of risk.

As an agent, explaining TCOR to a prospect can be a game-changer in terms of positioning yourself as a trusted advisor rather than just a salesperson. Here's how you can go about it:

Break It Down: Start by explaining that TCOR includes not just insurance premiums, but also administrative costs, loss control expenses, and even indirect costs like brand damage or reduced productivity.

Use Real-Life Examples: To make it more relatable, provide real-world examples or case studies where focusing on TCOR made a significant impact on a business, perhaps even saving it from potential ruin.

Show the Math: If possible, show them a basic calculation of how TCOR works, using figures they can relate to. You might even want to prepare a simplified TCOR analysis based on preliminary data about the prospect's company.

Explain the Benefits: Make it clear that a lower TCOR not only saves money but also can make their operations more efficient, reduce volatility, and make their business more attractive for partnerships, investors, and even future buyers.

Connect to Their Pain Points: If you've done your homework, you should know your prospect's primary business concerns. Align your knowledge of their business and reduce TCOR with these specific pain points.

By taking the time to educate your prospects about TCOR, you're doing more than just selling a policy; you're providing them with the tools they need to better understand their business. This not only makes you a valuable consultant to them but also sets the stage for a long-term relationship built on trust and mutual benefit.

So when you step into that meeting you secured through your consultative cold call, you're not just another salesperson trying to make a quick sale. You're a trusted advisor, there to educate the prospects and help them make a more informed decision. You discuss TCOR, help them understand their exposure, and offer tailored solutions that meet their specific needs. This not only sets you apart from competitors but also fosters a relationship that is far more likely to be long-term and mutually beneficial.

By leading with a consultative sales approach, you change the entire dynamic of the sales conversation. You give the client the tools they need to view their situation from a more informed perspective, empowering them to make decisions that will genuinely benefit their business. This is why consultative selling is superior: it doesn't just attract new clients—it creates loyal advocates for your services.

Understanding the Client's Business Model and Risk Profile

Understanding the Client's Business Model and Risk Profile: A Deep Dive Approach

In-Depth Research: Prior to any face-to-face interaction, it's vital to conduct thorough research on the prospective client's industry, market position, and key competitors. This involves more than just a quick Google search; it requires a deep dive into their annual reports, customer reviews, news articles, and social media mentions. Industry publications can offer insights into broader trends and challenges that the business might be facing. Understanding their revenue streams, operational costs, and financial stability will also provide you with a comprehensive view of their business model. The more you know about the intricacies of their operations, the better positioned you'll be to offer tailored advice.

Risk Assessment: The second pillar of the consultative sales approach involves a detailed risk assessment. Start by identifying the types of risks that are inherent to their industry. Are they in a sector that's heavily regulated, and thus, subject to compliance risks? Do they rely on a global supply chain, making them vulnerable to geopolitical instabilities? Or perhaps, given their business model, they face a higher level of cyber threats.

But the risk assessment shouldn't just be industry-specific; it should also consider the general business risks any enterprise might face, such as property damage or employee liability. A thorough risk assessment will categorize these risks into various buckets like operational, financial, strategic, and hazard risks.

Once you have a list of potential risks, the next step is to evaluate the severity and likelihood of each risk occurring. This will often involve a mixture of qualitative and quantitative analysis, sometimes utilizing tools like SWOT analysis or risk heat maps. You'll also need to understand the client's existing risk management measures. Are they adequate? What are the gaps? Where can enhancements be made?

After this comprehensive risk assessment, you'll be equipped to offer insurance solutions that are directly aligned with the client's specific risks and business objectives. Instead of a one-size-fits-all policy, you can suggest customized coverages, risk mitigation strategies, and even long-term plans for risk management, thereby demonstrating your value as a consultative partner rather than a mere vendor.

Both in-depth research and risk assessment lay the groundwork for a meaningful consultation. They enable you to speak the client's language, anticipate their questions, and proactively offer solutions. By doing your homework and focusing on their unique risk profile, you elevate the sales conversation from a transactional exchange to a strategic discussion, which is far more likely to result in a long-term business relationship.

Mastering the Art of Active Listening in Sales: Asking Questions That Unlock Value

The Power of Open-ended Questions: A consultative sales approach starts with opening the floor for a broader discussion. Open-ended questions like "Can you describe your current risk management strategy?" or "How do you handle compliance issues?" provide you with valuable insights while encouraging the client to share more. These questions also serve as conversation starters that can organically lead to other important topics. They allow clients to express their needs and concerns in their own words, giving you a more nuanced understanding of what they're looking for.

The Art of Reflective Listening: After the client responds, practice reflective listening by paraphrasing or summarizing what they've just said. For example, if a client says, "We've struggled with supply chain disruptions," you might respond with, "So, if I understand correctly, supply chain stability has been a significant issue for you." This does two things: it shows that you are actively engaged in the conversation and are not just waiting for your turn to speak, and it ensures that you've correctly understood their concerns or needs. It serves as a double-check mechanism and lays the foundation for trust and clarity.

The Importance of Not Interrupting: In the heat of a sales conversation, it's easy to start formulating responses or solutions while the client is still speaking. However, this can lead to premature or inappropriate solutions and shows a lack of respect for the client's perspective. The importance of allowing the client to fully articulate their thoughts cannot be overstated. It's not merely polite but also strategic, as sometimes the most crucial details emerge at the end of a longer explanation. Active listening is a critical skill for sales professionals. In a sales call, the goal is to understand the prospect's needs and offer solutions. When salespeople interrupt or dominate the conversation, they may miss essential details about the client's requirements and pain points.

Interrupting a client can create a negative perception, making the client feel undervalued or unheard. It can also hinder the rapport-building process, which is foundational to establishing trust and closing deals.

Moreover, the illusion of a successful meeting can arise if the salesperson did most of the talking. This is a dangerous misconception. If the salesperson is speaking more than the client, it's likely they're not gaining the insights needed to tailor their pitch or offer the best solutions. A sales call where the potential client does most of the talking, while expressing their needs, challenges, and aspirations, will provide a better foundation for the salesperson to position their product or service effectively.

While being articulate and persuasive is essential in sales, it's equally crucial to listen actively and avoid interruption. This ensures that salespeople capture critical insights, build rapport, and can provide the most relevant solutions for their prospects.

The Value of Seeking Clarifications: If a client's response is vague or packed with industry jargon that you're not familiar with, don't hesitate to ask for clarification. Questions like, "Could you elaborate on that point?" or "What do you mean by XYZ?" signal that you're not just listening to them, but you're genuinely interested in understanding their specific situation. This approach is essential for tailoring your solutions with pinpoint accuracy. It also provides the opportunity to dive deeper into issues that the client may not have initially considered critical but are underlying pain points needing solutions.

Active listening, encapsulated by these four points, elevates your sales process from a transactional activity to a consultative dialogue. It transforms you from a simple vendor into a trusted advisor, making it more likely that you'll not only close the sale but also develop a long-term relationship with the client. By asking the right questions and truly listening to the answers, you create a feedback loop that continually refines your offerings and aligns them more closely with your clients' evolving needs.

Tom was an ambitious commercial insurance producer who had just heard about Jorge, the owner of a thriving manufacturing business. Knowing that manufacturers often deal with complex risk profiles, Tom suspected that Jorge might be interested in insurance solutions that do more than just cover the basics.

Tom had never reached out to Jorge before, so this was a cold call in the truest sense. But he wasn't flying blind. Before dialing Jorge's number, Tom researched the company extensively to understand its size, services, and potential risks. With this information in hand, Tom crafted a compelling value proposition focused on Total Cost of Risk (TCOR), something he felt would resonate with a business owner dealing with various types of exposures.

Finally, he picked up the phone and dialed.

"Hello, this is Jorge."

"Hi Jorge, my name is Tom. I specialize in commercial insurance with a focus on manufacturing companies like yours. Do you have a few minutes to discuss some strategies that could significantly lower your Total Cost of Risk?"

Jorge was immediately intrigued. Most calls he received from insurance salespeople were scripted monologues about premiums. "You have two minutes," he said, slightly amused.

"Great, thank you, Jorge. Most insurance companies in your sector are focused on quoting premiums, but that's only the tip of the iceberg. What if I told you that I could help you not just with competitive premiums but also with reducing other costs like administrative and potential losses? All these elements contribute to your Total Cost of Risk. Could we perhaps set up a meeting to discuss this in detail?"

By framing the conversation around TCOR, Tom was able to turn what might have been a quick dismissal into a scheduled appointment.

"Certainly, Tom, you've got my attention. Let's meet."

Days later, when they finally met, Tom applied active listening techniques and consultative selling strategies, positioning himself not just as an insurance agent but as a trusted advisor. He used open-ended questions to encourage Jorge to share detailed responses about his business concerns and fears. He also employed reflective listening to ensure clarity and demonstrate his genuine interest in Jorge's unique challenges. And so began a partnership that was likely to meet the necessary criteria to last a long time, all initiated by a strategic cold call that shifted the focus from price to value.

As Tom hung up the phone after confirming the date of their next meeting to review customized insurance solutions, he realized the power of a well-executed cold call. He didn't close a sale on that initial call; that wasn't the goal. Instead, he opened a door, one that led to a meeting, a meaningful dialogue, and potentially a long-term client relationship. It was a lesson in the efficacy of targeted, value-based outreach, and one that he would carry with him throughout his career.

Tom was eager to get to know Jorge. Unlike most business owners, who viewed insurance as just another checkbox on their long list of responsibilities, Jorge was actively shopping

The Ultimate Advantage

for quotes. He was dissatisfied with his current coverage but was unsure what he wanted in a new policy or advisor. Tom knew this meeting was his chance to transform Jorge from a one-time shopper to a lifetime client.

The meeting kicked off with Tom using open-ended questions to gauge the landscape. "Jorge, could you walk me through some of the challenges you've been experiencing with your current insurance coverage?"

Jorge leaned back in his chair, "You know, Tom, it's like we're throwing money into a black hole. Our premiums are high, and every time we have a claim, it's a nightmare. I don't think our current agent even understands what we do here."

Seizing the moment to employ reflective listening, Tom responded, "So you're facing high premiums and poor claim experiences, all while feeling your agent is out of touch with the specialized nature of your business. Is that correct?"

"Yes, you nailed it," Jorge confirmed.

Tom knew the significance of allowing the client to freely express their concerns. He took the opportunity to let Jorge speak, not interrupting but prompting him with nods and affirmative expressions.

Jorge continued, "This business isn't just about machinery and employees. It's about managing volatile material costs, dealing with supply chain interruptions, and ensuring worker safety. These things keep me up at night."

Tom knew it was time to seek clarification, "You mentioned volatile material costs. How does that typically impact your business?"

"We have to sometimes alter production schedules, and that can put us in a bind. We might even have to take out short-term loans to cover it," Jorge explained.

The Ultimate Advantage

"Thank you for that insight," Tom said, tapping his pen on his notepad. "The details matter when I'm considering the right insurance solutions to fit your needs."

As they explored these issues more, Tom brought up the concept of Total Cost of Risk (TCOR), a concept Jorge hadn't considered before.

"Jorge, have you ever thought of insurance not as a mere expenditure but as a strategic investment? TCOR includes your premiums but goes beyond to consider administrative costs, potential losses, even the softer costs like reputational damage. By addressing these elements, the premium becomes a tool that can drive down your entire TCOR over time."

Jorge perked up, "I hadn't considered that. If you can help us not just insure against risks but manage them proactively, then that would be game-changing for us."

With a smile, Tom realized he'd accomplished his mission: he had shifted the conversation from a price-based comparison to a value-based partnership.

Jorge concluded, "Tom, I came into this meeting just shopping for quotes. But now, I'm looking for an advisor, a partner who can help us strategically reduce our total cost of risk over the years."

Tom had achieved his goal, not by selling a policy but by beginning a meaningful dialogue that would evolve into a long-term partnership. By implementing the principles of active listening and introducing a focus on TCOR, he positioned himself not just as an insurance sales associate but as a trusted business advisor. It was a relationship that would benefit both parties for years to come.

The End.

The Ultimate Advantage

> In this narrative, Tom successfully employed active listening and a consultative approach, combined with the strategic focus on TCOR, to change the buying criteria. The story illustrates how a true consultative approach can alter the client's perception from shopping for a commodity to investing in a long-term partnership. It's not just about lowering premiums, but about using insurance as a strategic tool to reduce the Total Cost of Risk over time.

The consultative sales approach is about partnership. By truly understanding the intricacies of your client's business and their risk profile, you position yourself as a trusted advisor, not just a salesperson. The result? Longer-lasting client relationships and more effective, tailored insurance solutions.

In the next chapters, we'll build on these foundations and delve into crafting compelling proposals, managing objections, and closing deals effectively.

Chapter 5: Crafting the Conceptual Proposal

The Transition from Detail-Heavy to Conceptual

In the commercial insurance industry, the traditional route involves presenting a detailed, often cumbersome proposal. But what if you could be more effective with a conceptual approach? This chapter will guide you on how to create a proposal that resonates with your prospects at an emotional and intellectual level.

In the commercial insurance landscape, a Conceptual Proposal serves as a roadmap outlining the insurance services and risk management strategies that an agent offers to a prospective client. Unlike a formal proposal, which provides in-depth details such as policy terms, limits, and premiums, a Conceptual Proposal is more like a high-level overview aimed at presenting the value an agent can add to the client's business. Essentially, it gives a snapshot of the solutions designed to meet the unique needs and challenges faced by the client's business.

Importance of a Conceptual Proposal

The conceptual proposal comes into play when agents want to take a consultative approach. This strategy means that the agent is not merely selling insurance products but actually offering customized solutions that contribute to reducing the client's Total Cost of Risk (TCOR). By presenting a Conceptual Proposal, agents have the opportunity to show prospects that they understand the intricacies of their business and industry, thus positioning themselves as trusted advisors rather than mere salespeople.

Advantages of Using a Conceptual Proposal

Creates a Partnership Dynamic: A well-crafted conceptual proposal makes the client feel like you are partnering with them to solve their problems, not just selling them a product.

Facilitates Consultative Selling: It allows for a consultative sales approach, where understanding and solving the client's unique challenges become the focus.

Flexibility: Because it's a high-level overview, it's easier to adjust and tweak as you get more information from the prospect, thereby staying agile in your sales approach.

Presentation and Follow-up

The way you present the Conceptual Proposal is as crucial as its content. It should be professionally designed and may include visual aids like charts or graphs to make the information more accessible. Digital formats are often preferable, as they can be easily shared and amended.

After delivering the Conceptual Proposal, follow-up is key. It's not just about getting a "yes" or "no;" it's also an opportunity to refine your proposal based on the feedback. Did the prospect find your risk assessment accurate? Are there additional services they'd like included? These insights are invaluable for customizing your ultimate formal proposal.

In summary, a Conceptual Proposal serves as a foundational document in commercial insurance sales, offering a flexible and strategic tool that can adapt to a constantly changing business environment. It puts the emphasis on the agent's expertise and consultative role, paving the way for a trust-based, long-term relationship with the client.

Structuring the Proposal:

Introduction and Executive Summary

The proposal should begin with a concise yet comprehensive introduction and executive summary. This section serves as a roadmap, outlining what the proposal will cover and establishing the significance of the document for the client. Here, you set the stage for the in-depth analysis and tailored solutions that will follow.

Understanding Business Challenges: Highlighting Pain Points

This is the section where you make it clear that you've done your homework. Detail the challenges, bottlenecks, and specific risks that are pertinent to the client's industry. The aim is not merely to list the challenges but to create a sense of urgency by underlining the impact of these issues if not adequately addressed.

Risk Assessment

After laying out the client's specific challenges and pain points, your next step is to conduct a risk assessment. This should cover both general and industry-specific risks. The more comprehensive your assessment, the more you prove your worth as a consultant, not just a vendor.

Suggested Solutions: Presenting Solutions

While your solutions might encompass an array of complex insurance products and underwriting details, it's crucial to keep the proposal at a high level. The objective is to relate each proposed solution directly to a pain point you've already highlighted. Instead of listing product features, focus on benefits and outcomes.

Value-Added Services

This is your opportunity to differentiate yourself from the competition. Discuss any value-added services like real-time claims assistance, risk assessment audits, or specialized customer service that you offer. These services often act as tiebreakers when clients are comparing options.

Timeline

Include a general yet structured timeline indicating the phases of risk assessment, implementation, review, and so on. This gives your prospect an idea of what to expect and when.

Next Steps: Benefits and Call to Action

End by summarizing the benefits: a future where risks are strategically managed, allowing the business to focus on growth and profitability. This is your final pitch and call to action. Clearly outline what the client needs to do next to initiate this transformative process.

Leveraging Storytelling for Maximum Impact

Narrative Flow

While a proposal is fundamentally a business document, crafting it with a narrative flow can increase its impact multifold. Develop your proposal like a storyline, leading the client from their current challenges to a future where they experience significantly fewer risks and more peace of mind.

Relatable Examples

Anecdotes and case studies (anonymized to protect confidentiality) can be powerful tools. If you can include stories of past clients who faced similar challenges and how your solutions made a real difference, you make your proposal not just persuasive but also relatable.

By implementing these elements thoughtfully, your conceptual proposal will not merely be an offering of insurance products; it becomes a compelling narrative that demonstrates your deep understanding of the client's needs and the unique value you bring to addressing them.

Tom adjusted his tie and took a deep breath before walking into Jorge's office. Concerned about how to successfully grow his manufacturing company, Jorge was accustomed to insurance agents coming through his door, but Tom was confident that today would be different. Armed with a conceptual proposal focused on Jorge's specific business challenges and potential solutions, Tom was ready.

"Good to see you again, Jorge," Tom said with a warm smile, offering a firm handshake.

"And you, Tom. What do you have for me today?" Jorge asked, settling into his chair.

Tom opened his laptop and began his presentation. "Let's dive right in. I've developed a conceptual proposal tailored precisely to your company's unique risk profile."

Introduction and Executive Summary

Tom started, "We're going to review how we can identify and manage the specific risks associated with your manufacturing business."

Jorge nodded, intrigued.

Understanding of Business Challenges: Highlighting Pain Points

"We've thoroughly researched the challenges your manufacturing business faces, from supply chain disruptions to safety hazards," Tom outlined, capturing Jorge's attention.

Risk Assessment

The Ultimate Advantage

"Using that research, we conducted a detailed risk assessment, capturing both your industry-specific and general business risks," Tom continued.

"Very thorough," Jorge remarked.

Suggested Solutions: Presenting Solutions

"Exactly. So, let's talk about strategic solutions to mitigate these risks, rather than just diving into policy details," Tom proposed.

Value-Added Services

"We also offer value-added services like 24/7 claims support and regular safety audits, which significantly differentiate us from the competition," Tom emphasized.

"Very beneficial," Jorge noted.

Timeline

"Here's our proposed timeline for implementing these risk management strategies," Tom elaborated, displaying a well-structured roadmap.

Next Steps: Benefits and Call to Action

"To summarize," Tom concluded with conviction, "we're not just offering you an insurance policy. We're offering a business solution that could be crucial to advancing your strategic objectives."

Leveraging Storytelling for Maximum Impact

"And to bring it all home, I've included case studies from other manufacturing clients. They've seen both reduced risks and lowered costs with our services," Tom wrapped up.

"Tom, you've clearly done your research," Jorge said, visibly impressed.

The Ultimate Advantage

The Key Call to Action: Asking for the BOR

Seizing the moment, Tom leaned in. "Jorge, based on what we've discussed today, I strongly believe we're exceptionally well-positioned to improve your risk management and drive down your total costs. I'll need a Broker of Record letter from you. This will enable us to begin work immediately and initiate the strategies we've discussed today. Are you ready to move forward?"

Jorge looked at Tom, sensed the confidence, and felt reassured. "Yes," he said. "Let's do this."

Tom closed his laptop with a sense of triumph. He had succeeded in not only presenting a convincing proposal but also in positioning himself as a trusted business consultant. The Broker of Record letter would be more than a formality; it was the key to an impactful, long-term partnership.

Chapter 6: Mastering the Art of Presentation

From Paper to Persuasion

When presenting a proposal in the world of commercial insurance, it's essential to understand that you're not just relaying information; you're engaging in a highly strategic form of persuasion. Every word uttered, every slide presented, and every question posed serves a purpose. It all aims to lead the client toward recognizing the value you bring and choosing to work with you. And that's a crucial distinction; it's not just about selling a product or service, but about selling yourself as a trusted advisor.

The journey toward this moment of persuasion starts from the very first touchpoint, often a cold call. The effectiveness of your proposal is shaped by how well you managed to initiate the relationship, establish trust, and open the lines of communication. By capturing the prospect's attention initially, you've already laid the groundwork for a compelling presentation.

Active listening plays an enormous role throughout the process, especially in the earlier conversations or meetings. It allows you to gain a deep understanding of the client's needs, concerns, and objections. The art of asking the right questions and genuinely listening to the responses provides the raw material for a presentation that addresses the client's pain points precisely and offers targeted solutions.

The Ultimate Advantage

This sort of listening helps you tailor your proposal, making the client feel understood and valued.

During the presentation, everything you've learned comes to the forefront. You address specific pain points that you've uncovered, showing that you understand the challenges and risks unique to the client's business. You're not making assumptions or offering one-size-fits-all solutions but delivering targeted recommendations based on in-depth research and understanding. This knowledge allows you to handle objections proactively, by providing answers to questions the client may have or concerns they might raise.

Your research also equips you to speak authoritatively on how your solutions can positively impact their Total Cost of Risk (TCOR) and not just offer cheaper premiums. Changing the client's objective from shopping for a cheaper price to seeking a trusted advisor is a key moment in the persuasive process. It shows that you're not just another salesperson but an industry expert who can bring value to their business.

Effective persuasion also includes employing storytelling techniques. You may use client success stories to make abstract concepts more concrete. Narratives resonate with people and make your proposal more relatable and compelling. Telling a compelling "story" about how the client's situation will improve by working with you can be the emotional nudge that pushes them towards saying yes.

You can also use the power of social proof to reinforce your points. Testimonials from other satisfied clients can strengthen your case, providing external validation that what you're proposing actually works. It's an added layer of reassurance that addresses any lingering objections the client might have.

Towards the end of your presentation, when you believe you've sufficiently handled objections and built value, make your Call to Action (CTA). Your CTA needs to be strong, clear, and direct, telling the client exactly what you want them to do next. The information you've gathered along the way, from the initial cold call to the last meeting, should inform how you phrase this critical component of your proposal.

Finally, remember that persuasion is a two-way street. While you aim to persuade the client, you also need to allow room for them to "sell" themselves on working with you. This can happen when you effectively lead them to connect the dots, to see how your solutions address their unique pain points, and to envision a future where they're better off because they chose to work with you.

From the first cold call to the presentation of the conceptual proposal, every step is an exercise in strategic persuasion. By doing your research, actively listening, tailoring your proposal, handling objections, employing storytelling, and presenting a compelling call to action, you're not just relaying information. You're leading your prospect through a decision-making journey, the end goal of which is a beneficial partnership for both parties.

Proposal Presentation Techniques

Mastering the art of proposal presentation requires dedication and practice, just like any other skilled endeavor. Unfortunately, many insurance agents underestimate the value of rehearsal, if their eloquence or the strength of their proposal alone will make the sale. This is a costly mistake; when it comes to impactful presentations, practice doesn't just make perfect—it makes persuasive.

The first element to emphasize is practice. If athletes spend hours each day practicing to improve their performance,

The Ultimate Advantage

and soldiers run through meticulous drills to prepare for high-stakes missions, why shouldn't a sales agent also practice? Knowing your proposal inside and out, anticipating possible questions, and having answers at the ready can make the difference between securing a client and losing them. Just as you wouldn't enter an athletic competition or a military mission without adequate preparation, you shouldn't walk into a proposal presentation without thorough practice.

When practicing, it's crucial to review your proposal in both paper and digital formats. While paper allows you to physically markup points of emphasis or places where you anticipate questions, digital formats offer the advantage of being accessible from multiple devices, making it easier to practice anytime, anywhere. Familiarizing yourself with both formats ensures that you are prepared for any situation, whether that involves projecting your proposal on a screen or distributing hard copies to meeting attendees.

In addition to solitary practice, consider engaging a coach or a trusted colleague to "war-game" your presentation. This exercise involves having your coach play the role of a potential client who offers objections or asks questions. This method of role-playing can help you anticipate a wider range of questions and prepare responses for them. It also provides an opportunity to refine your persuasion techniques and improve your presentation flow.

Another highly effective practice technique is recording yourself. In the heat of a presentation, you may not notice verbal ticks, pacing issues, or points where you lack clarity. By reviewing a recording, you can identify these areas for improvement that you may not have otherwise noticed. It can also help you gauge the length of your presentation, ensuring that you cover all the necessary points within the time constraints of a typical client meeting.

The Ultimate Advantage

Moving on to the presentation itself, visuals are crucial. They serve as complementary elements that can significantly enhance your spoken words. Slides, charts, and infographics not only make your presentation more engaging but also help in breaking down complex points. A well-placed visual can clarify or emphasize a point more succinctly than a lengthy explanation.

While visuals are valuable aids, the core of your presentation is still the dialogue you establish with your potential client. Therefore, involving your audience is crucial. Encourage questions throughout your presentation, not just at the end. This interactive approach ensures that your audience is engaged and allows you to address any misunderstandings or objections in real-time.

The psychology behind involving your audience is quite straightforward. People tend to engage more deeply with material when they feel they are part of a dialogue rather than passive recipients of a monologue. Each question you entertain and satisfactorily answer also adds a brick to the edifice of trust and credibility you're building throughout your presentation.

An impactful proposal presentation is a product of numerous elements—meticulous preparation, tactical practice, effective use of visuals, and active audience involvement. Just as you wouldn't expect to win a sports competition without rigorous training, succeeding in the high-stakes arena of proposal presentations demands its own form of disciplined practice and preparation.

So, the next time you're on the brink of walking into a presentation without adequate preparation, think about the athletes on the field or the soldiers on a mission. They wouldn't dream of performing without intensive practice; why should you?

Handling Objections

Managing objections effectively is crucial during the proposal presentation stage, as it not only clarifies any uncertainties but also bolsters your credibility. Let's break down some common objections and ways to address them:

Price Concerns: Cost is often the elephant in the room. When a client brings up the issue of price, steer the conversation toward long-term value and benefits. For instance, you could counter with, "I understand budget constraints are a real concern. However, opting for the cheapest plan can result in inadequate coverage when you most need it. Our proposal aims to give you the best value, covering all essential risks without any hidden gaps." This reframing puts the emphasis on long-term security over short-term savings.

Coverage Concerns: If your client raises issues about the scope of your coverage, this is your opportunity to shine. Point out specific weaknesses or gaps in their existing coverage and how your proposed plan remedies those. For example: "You mentioned your current policy doesn't cover 'X,' which is a typical risk in your industry. Our proposal comprehensively addresses this by including 'Y' feature."

Relationship with the Incumbent Agent: It's not uncommon for clients to have a longstanding relationship with their current agent. In these cases, try to delicately pivot the conversation to the client's evolving needs. You could say, "I respect your loyalty to your current agent. However, as your business grows, so do its complexities and risks. Our specialized focus in your industry] means we can offer a new layer of expertise and risk mitigation."

Resistance to Broker of Record (BOR): Signing a BOR is often a sticking point for many clients because it feels like a significant commitment. It's vital to educate them on the process and its importance. For example: "Signing a Broker of Record allows us to act on your behalf immediately. I should also note that your current agent has already been compensated for this policy year. We only get paid when the policy renews, effectively letting you evaluate our services without additional cost until then. And if at any point you feel we haven't lived up to our promises, you can always revert back by signing another BOR." Remember for you as a producer this is potentially new business from a new client. From the client's perspective this is their renewal. Becoming the Broker of Record allows you to present the client on the most favorable terms to potential carriers.

By understanding the nature of these objections and offering compelling, fact-based responses, you not only demonstrate your expertise but also build trust. Providing clear and insightful answers is key to transforming these objections into opportunities for deeper engagement and, ultimately, a fruitful business relationship.

Robbie had gone through his proposal with a fine-tooth comb, preparing for his meeting with Carmen, the owner of a local gymnastics' facility. When he walked into her brightly lit office, he felt the adrenaline of a well-prepared agent ready to address any concerns or objections Carmen might have.

After a warm greeting and some small talk, Robbie delved right into the core of the presentation. He outlined the pain points specific to the sports and recreational industry—everything from athlete injuries to equipment liabilities. Then, he presented his customized insurance solutions aimed at mitigating these challenges. Robbie concluded this section of the meeting by sharing an anonymized case study of another gymnastics facility that had successfully reduced risks through his proposed changes.

The Ultimate Advantage

"Your proposal sounds comprehensive, Robbie, but the cost seems high, especially given our budget constraints," Carmen said, voicing her first objection.

Robbie had expected this. "I understand your budget concerns, Carmen. But consider the high costs associated with even a single liability case, which could run to the hundreds of thousands. Our plans are crated to be a long-term investment to protect your facility and its future."

"True," Carmen mused, "but I've worked with my current agent for years. It's hard to think about switching."

Robbie seized the opportunity to highlight his agency's unique offering. "I absolutely respect long-standing business relationships, Carmen. However, our agency has a specialized practice group focusing solely on sports and recreational facilities. We offer a unique level of expertise in this area that can add significant value to your existing coverage."

Carmen seemed to ponder this, then hesitantly asked about the Broker of Record (BOR). "It's a big step to sign a BOR. What if things don't go as planned?"

Addressing her concerns directly, Robbie said, "The BOR allows us to start working on your behalf immediately, Carmen, especially in preparing for the renewal of your policy. We'll have access to all markets, allowing us to negotiate better terms for you. And remember, your current agent has already been paid for this year. We won't receive compensation until the policy renews, so it's like you're getting extra services for no additional cost. If, at any point, you're not satisfied with our services, you can switch back by signing a new BOR."

Carmen nodded, finally appearing convinced. "Alright, Robbie, you've done a good job addressing my concerns. Let's move forward."

The Ultimate Advantage

As Robbie left the meeting, he felt a sense of professional pride. Not only had he prepared a strong proposal, but he had also effectively neutralized each of Carmen's objections. It was a win borne out of preparation, specialized expertise, and the ability to pivot the conversation from fears to actionable solutions.

Closing Strategies

The **"Assumptive Close"** is one of the most straightforward closing techniques, often used when the client has shown strong buying signals throughout the sales process. In this strategy, the agent simply acts as if the client has already decided to purchase, moving on to logistics or next steps. For example, an agent might say, "So, let's start the paperwork so you can have coverage starting next month?" This approach minimizes the pressure and encourages a smooth transition to closing the sale.

The **"Summary Close"** involves recapping the main points that were discussed during the sales meeting, especially those where the client showed significant interest or concern. By summarizing the pain points addressed, benefits offered, and the added value provided, the agent helps the client review the whole picture. An agent could say, "We've talked about how our policy addresses your unique risks, offers 24/7 customer support, and comes with risk management consultations. Does this solution meet your needs?"

The **"Sharp Angle Close"** is useful when the client has a specific request or concern that hasn't been addressed. The

The Ultimate Advantage

agent agrees to meet this request but immediately asks for the sale in return. For example, if a client asks for a specific add-on or discount, the agent might reply, "I can include that extra coverage at no additional cost. Can we move forward with the agreement now?"

The **"Alternative Choice Close"** gives the client a choice between two options, both of which result in a sale. The aim here is to eliminate the "yes or no" nature of the decision and make the client feel empowered. For instance, an agent might ask, "Would you like to start your new policy at the beginning of next month, or would mid-month work better for you?"

The **"Urgency Close"** involves making the offer time-sensitive to encourage immediate action. Agents using this strategy must be careful not to pressure the client overly. The key is to make the urgency believable and relevant. "Our discounted rates for new customers for our loss control services are only available until the end of this month. I'd hate for you to miss out on this offer," is an example of how this could be presented.

The **"Trial Close"** is a softer approach to gauge where the client stands. It involves asking open-ended questions aimed at revealing the client's readiness to move forward. For example, an agent might ask, "How do you feel about what we've discussed so far?" or "Does this solution seem like it would meet your needs?" Based on the answers, the agent can decide whether to proceed to the final close.

The **"Emotion-Logic Close"** is a two-step process. First, appeal to your client's emotional needs ("Imagine the peace of mind you'll have knowing that all your risks covered"). Then follow up immediately with logical reasoning ("We offer the most comprehensive coverage at a very competitive price"). This two-pronged approach can be compelling because it appeals to both the heart and mind.

The **"If I Could, Would You?"** Close turns a client's objection into a condition for closing the sale. For instance, if a client says the premium is too high, the agent could respond, "If I could find a way to fit this into your budget, would you be willing to move forward today?" By resolving the objection, this strategy opens the door to finalizing the deal.

These closing techniques can be used in different scenarios depending on the client's behavior, objections, and needs. The key is always to keep the client's best interests in mind while guiding them toward a decision that benefits both parties.

Chapter 7: The Power of BORs (Broker of Record Letters)

The Game-Changer

The power of Broker of Record Letters (BORs) in commercial insurance is often underestimated. These formal agreements can be game changing for how insurance agents interact with both clients and carriers. Far from just another piece of paperwork, a well-executed BOR can redefine the dynamics of client relationships, offering a level of exclusivity that significantly benefits both parties.

Many agents shy away from the topic of BORs, often out of fear or lack of understanding. Some are concerned that suggesting a BOR may make them appear overly aggressive or even presumptuous. This fear often stems from a lack of familiarity with the process and the potential administrative challenges involved. However, what they fail to realize is that a BOR serves as a strong statement of trust and commitment between the client and the broker.

When a client signs a Broker of Record Letter, they give the broker exclusive rights to represent their insurance interests. This puts the agent in a strong position to negotiate the best terms with insurance carriers. In essence, you're not just selling your services to the client; you're also "selling" the client's risk profile to the carrier, making a case for why they should be offered the best possible terms.

In an industry where agencies often retain up to 90% of their accounts, the odds are generally stacked against new entrants. Getting a new client often means displacing an incumbent broker, which is a tall order given these high retention rates. However, a BOR can change all that. The moment you secure a BOR, you signal to the insurance carrier that you are the client's chosen representative, thus increasing your bargaining power substantially.

From the perspective of the underwriter, a broker armed with a BOR is more than just a quote request; they represent a certainty. Normally, when carriers receive quote requests, they know there's only a small chance—about 10%—of the new agent will win the business, thanks to the industry's high retention rates. A BOR transforms this dynamic; you go from being a long shot to a sure bet, making it more likely that the underwriter will provide a competitive quote.

But holding a BOR isn't enough; the quality of your submission to the carrier also matters greatly. A detailed, accurate submission shows the carrier that you have a deep understanding of the client's needs and are therefore more likely to retain the business in the long term. This, combined with a BOR, becomes your ultimate advantage.

One of the challenges brokers often face is explaining the benefits of a BOR to a potential client. It's not just about that moment of signing; it's a commitment that allows you to take immediate action. For instance, it lets you start preparations for renewals or carry out risk assessments, offering a level of proactive service that many clients may not have experienced before.

And this is where the real power of a BOR shines. In a field as competitive as commercial insurance, every advantage counts. By controlling the account and the conversation with the carrier, you greatly increase the chances of crafting the perfect policy for your client, providing a level of service that stands head and shoulders above the competition.

In summary, the utility of a BOR extends far beyond its basic function. It can be the secret weapon that sets you apart in the intensely competitive world of commercial insurance. By mastering the art of obtaining and effectively using BORs, you can redefine your approach to building client and carrier relationships, securing a crucial edge in your professional journey.

Navigating BOR Ethics

Navigating the complex landscape of Broker of Record Letters (BORs) in commercial insurance isn't just a matter of strategy or savvy negotiation; it's also an exercise in ethical responsibility. Ethical considerations underpin every stage of the BOR process—from the initial conversation with a prospective client to the ongoing service commitments after securing the account.

Transparency serves as the cornerstone of ethical BOR navigation. A transparent approach starts with laying out a clear roadmap for your prospective clients, explaining what a BOR is, how it alters the client-broker dynamic, and the immediate and long-term implications of signing one. While a BOR gives an agent exclusive rights to negotiate on behalf of a client, the client needs to understand what they're agreeing to. For instance, some may think signing a BOR means they're locked into a contractual relationship for an extended period when, in fact, most BORs have terms that allow for relatively easy termination by either party.

Equally important is the principle of avoiding undue pressure. While it's natural to advocate for your services passionately, it's crucial that the enthusiasm doesn't cross into coercion. Clients should feel they're making an informed decision when signing a BOR, not that they're being pressured into a corner. The aim should be to enable the client to make a conscious decision based on the merits of your services, and the value you bring to the table, rather than a sense of urgency you've artificially inflated.

Once you've acquired a BOR through transparent and pressure-free means, it's time to discuss service commitment. Obtaining a BOR isn't the endgame; rather, it marks the beginning of a relationship defined by a heightened level of service expectation. It's not merely a "win" in your column; it's a solemn responsibility to provide your client with the best service possible. It's crucial to see this as an ongoing commitment rather than a one-time transaction.

This commitment means you need to get to work immediately. Gone are the days when a BOR was a "sign it and forget it" document. In today's hyper-competitive insurance landscape, resting on your laurels after obtaining a BOR is perhaps the most damaging thing you can do. Your new client will expect—and rightfully so—that you'll now pull out all the stops to represent their interests to the best of your ability. That's the commitment you've implicitly agreed to when they handed you the exclusive right to represent them.

What does this work entail? The first item on your to-do list should be to start marketing the account right away. With a BOR in hand, you have a stronger hand to play with insurance carriers. This is the time to build out a comprehensive submission for underwriters, one that not only lists the facts but also tells a compelling story about why this particular client deserves favorable terms. But remember, this should align with all the promises you've made. The worst outcome would be for the client to feel that your services don't align with your initial pitch, leading to broken trust and, ultimately, a terminated BOR.

Every promise you made during the courting phase—whether it was about getting better premiums, enhancing coverage, or improving risk management practices—now comes into sharp focus. This is the phase where you need to deliver on every single one of those promises, thereby transforming the theoretical value proposition you offered into tangible benefits.

And herein lies the essence of BOR ethics. Transparency ensures the client knows what they're signing up for, and a steadfast service commitment ensures they get the value they were promised. In fulfilling these three pillars, you're not just doing right by your client; you're also strengthening your own position in a market where reputation is invaluable.

Navigating BOR ethics is not just about securing a business advantage; it's about laying the foundation for a lasting, fruitful relationship with your client. As in many areas of life and business, the right thing to do is also the smart thing to do. Upholding ethical standards in the BOR process ensures you're building relationships on a bedrock of mutual trust and shared value, setting the stage for long-term success for both parties.

With these strategies in hand, you're better equipped to navigate the commercial insurance landscape, from crafting persuasive proposals to securing your position with BORs.

The Ultimate Advantage

The subsequent chapters will delve into advanced techniques and the evolving world of commercial insurance.

Jacob, an experienced commercial insurance underwriter, scanned through his emails on a typical Wednesday afternoon. He was surprised to find two intriguing submissions for manufacturing risks, both with an estimated annual premium of around $100,000. On the one hand, there was Anthony, a well-known agent from a small local shop, recognized for his meticulousness and punctuality. On the other hand, there was Matt, a producer from another agency who claimed to have secured the Broker of Record (BOR) for a similar account.

Anthony's submission was complete and neatly arranged. It included all the ACCORD forms and comprehensive loss runs. Jacob had worked with him before and knew that the agent's attention to detail would make the underwriting process a lot smoother.

But Matt's email caught his eye for a different reason. Matt had the BOR, a powerful document that effectively guaranteed that he controlled the account. Matt mentioned that the account was currently with another carrier and asked Jacob if he could "sharpen his pencil," hinting at a need for competitive pricing. He wanted not just matching coverage but also an add-on for cyber liability. Matt promised to send over the complete submission if Jacob expressed interest.

Jacob paused to consider his options. While Anthony's submission was impressive and straightforward, he couldn't ignore the power of Matt's BOR. With the BOR in hand, Matt wasn't just shopping around; he had the authority to change carriers, offering Jacob a legitimate shot at securing the account. And it wasn't just about potential business. From an underwriter's perspective, a BOR symbolizes a deeper level of commitment, changing the dynamics of

The Ultimate Advantage

carrier negotiations and making Jacob's proposition to his internal team much stronger.

Additionally, Matt's request for specific pricing and enhanced coverages like cyber signaled a more intricate, tailored policy—exactly the kind of business that could showcase Jacob's underwriting skills. On the other hand, even if Anthony's submission was immaculate, there was no guarantee that he would win the business. After all, he was probably competing against other agencies.

Conventional wisdom would point toward prioritizing Anthony's submission because of its completeness and the agent's reputation for being detail oriented. But the world of underwriting isn't just about risk; it's about opportunities. And Matt's BOR was a significant opportunity that was too good to pass up.

Jacob decided to email Matt first, expressing his interest and willingness to be competitive in terms of pricing and coverage options. Matt's response came quickly, delivering on his promise to send a comprehensive submission. Once he received it, Jacob fast-tracked the application through his internal process. The BOR was a game-changer; it not only made his case compelling to the decision-makers within his company but also opened the doors to crafting a specialized policy that could potentially serve as a template for similar risks.

Though he didn't neglect Anthony's submission, Jacob knew where his immediate interest lay. The BOR had tipped the scales, and for an underwriter looking to add value both to his portfolio and his company, the choice was clear.

In the commercial insurance world, opportunities come in many forms. For Jacob, a detail-oriented underwriter who weighed his options carefully, the power of a BOR made all the difference, offering a pathway not just to new business, but to a more complex and fulfilling underwriting challenge.

Chapter 8: Building Long-term Client Relationships

Beyond the Sale

Once the ink is dry on the policy, the real work of nurturing and cultivating the client relationship begins. The success of an insurance producer is not just measured by the number of sales but by the longevity and depth of their client relationships.

Building long-term client relationships in the commercial insurance sector goes far beyond the initial sale. Once a policy is signed, that's merely the first step in what should be a long and mutually beneficial partnership. After all, the insurance landscape is ever-changing, and the producer's role extends from being just a policy provider to a risk management consultant, a problem solver, and a trusted advisor.

The Ultimate Advantage

Firstly, let's talk about onboarding new clients, a crucial phase that sets the tone for the entire relationship. The onboarding process must be seamless, giving the client a glimpse of your efficiency and attention to detail. This process usually involves collecting all necessary documentation, setting up the client in your management system, and walking them through the policy's coverage and exclusions. But, more importantly, it should also involve an introduction to the service team who will be their primary contacts for claims, questions, and any other concerns. This team could consist of account managers, risk analysts, and customer service reps, each with a specific role in the client's journey. An introduction can be made via a scheduled video conference or, better yet, an in-person meeting, which can be a more potent relationship-building tool.

Service

Next, the schedule of service needs to be established and clearly communicated to the client. This schedule outlines when the client can expect different types of engagement from your team, from quarterly business reviews to annual policy renewals. Knowing what to expect and when to expect it goes a long way in building trust. After all, surprises are not something businesses appreciate, especially when it comes to their insurance needs.

A schedule of service is essentially a roadmap of your ongoing relationship with a client. It outlines not only what services you will provide but also when and how these services will be rendered. Having a formal schedule of service can set you apart from other agents in several keyways, primarily by demonstrating your commitment to transparency, professionalism, and a client-first approach.

The standard of service is equally critical. Setting expectations about service standards provides a yardstick by which your performance will be measured. Will there be quarterly check-ins? What's the promised turnaround time for queries or claims? Is there a dedicated account manager? All these details should be shared in black and white, preferably in a service-level agreement. Setting these benchmarks up front eliminates gray areas and sets the stage for a transparent relationship.

Now, a critical yet often overlooked aspect of client relationship management is education. Insurance policies can be complex, filled with industry jargon that the average business owner may not fully understand. Take the time to educate your clients on what exactly their policies cover, what they don't, and how to go about filing a claim should the need arise. This transforms you from a salesperson into a valuable advisor.

It's also important to have a system in place for regular communication that isn't necessarily tied to policy renewals or claims. Regular updates on industry trends, a monthly newsletter, or even a congratulatory note on the client's business milestones can keep the relationship warm and the lines of communication open.

Client reviews should be a structured process and not just a courtesy call. You need to assess what has changed in their risk profile and business needs since the last review. Any new acquisitions? Any entry into new markets or industries that come with their own sets of regulations and exposures? This is an opportunity for you to add value by identifying gaps in their current policies and suggesting modifications.

The concept of upselling or cross-selling should also be approached strategically. While these techniques can increase your revenue, they can also serve the client by providing a more comprehensive risk management solution. The key is timing and approach; you must have a deep understanding of their business cycle and risk profile to know when to introduce new coverage options.

Remember, relationship-building is not just a one-way street. It's also about gathering feedback from your clients. Client feedback helps you understand your strengths and areas that might need improvement. This can be done through periodic surveys or, more effectively, through one-on-one meetings.

Ultimately, long-term client relationships are built on a foundation of trust, added value, and consistent, high-quality service. Through well-executed onboarding processes, clear schedules and service standards, continuous engagement, and diligent follow-up, you can ensure that your client sees you as more than just a vendor. In a competitive marketplace, where products are often similar, your relationship with the client can become your most durable competitive advantage.

At its core, a schedule of services should provide a timeline for each critical touchpoint you have with your client. These touchpoints can range from the initial policy discussion and onboarding to periodic policy reviews, renewal timelines, and even scheduled educational webinars or check-ins. Here's what it might look like:

Initial Onboarding Meeting

Onboarding typically occurs within a week of the policy being signed. This meeting is crucial because it sets the tone for the entire client-agent relationship. The client should have an opportunity to meet the service team, making sure the client knows who to reach out to depending on their need During this meeting, you can also help the client set up any software platforms they'll be using to manage their policy, like a customer portal or risk management software. Additionally, this meeting offers an opportunity to walk through the policy in detail, ensuring that the client fully understands the coverages they've purchased and any obligations or responsibilities they may have.

Thirty-Day Check-in

This check-in serves as a pulse check on how things are going after the initial excitement of the onboarding process has settled. This is a more informal conversation where you confirm that the client is comfortable with the software tools and understands how to access their policy details. Additionally, you can address any questions or concerns that may have arisen during the first month. This quick but essential check-in can often nip problems in the bud before they escalate.

Quarterly Business Reviews

Every three months, a more detailed review should be conducted. This is not merely an overview of the policy but also an assessment of any changes in the client's business that might necessitate modifications in coverage. During these reviews, you can update risk assessments, discuss any new assets that need coverage, or talk about operational changes that could affect their insurance needs. These reviews are proactive measures to keep the policy in alignment with the client's changing business landscape.

Bi-annual Educational Webinars

Education is an essential part of risk management. Twice a year, offer webinars on topics like "Managing Business Risks" or "What's New in Commercial Insurance." These sessions should provide actionable advice and updates on trends or changes in the insurance market. They can also be a way to introduce clients to additional services or coverage they might not have considered.

Pre-renewal Meeting

Three months before the policy is due for renewal, a comprehensive pre-renewal meeting should be scheduled. The objective here is to review current coverages, discuss any changes in business operations, and begin preparing for the renewal process. This meeting helps to avoid the last-minute rush and ensures that the client has ample time to consider any changes or adjustments to their policy.

Renewal Strategy Session

A month before the policy renewal date, a focused Renewal Strategy Session should take place. Here you present the client with different renewal options, including any adjustments in premiums and additional coverage like cyber insurance. This is a critical decision-making point, and this meeting ensures the client has all the information they need.

Annual Risk Assessment

A yearly deep dive into the client's risk landscape should also be part of your service schedule. This could involve bringing in third-party experts for assessments on cybersecurity, workplace safety, or other specialized concerns. The findings often provide invaluable insights that inform both the client's risk management strategies and the types of coverage they may need in the future.

Client Satisfaction Survey

An annual or bi-annual survey can provide valuable feedback on your services and identify areas for improvement. Questions can range from the client's satisfaction with their policy to how helpful they find the educational content you provide.

Client Appreciation Events

Never underestimate the power of showing appreciation. Whether it's a small gift on the anniversary of your partnership or an exclusive invitation to a networking event, gestures like these can go a long way in solidifying your relationship with the client.

By having a well-defined schedule of services, you're not only keeping your client interactions organized and proactive but you're also demonstrating a level of professionalism and commitment that can set you apart from competitors.

Why does a formal schedule of service separate you from other agents? First, it clearly demonstrates your commitment to organization and forward planning. Many agents are reactive, dealing with issues as they arise. While this might suffice for some clients, many businesses appreciate the ability to anticipate future actions and prepare for them.

Second, it also provides a certain level of transparency. It tells the client exactly what they can expect from you and when. This not only builds trust but also allows the client to hold you accountable to a set standard, reducing misunderstandings and disagreements down the line.

Third, having a structured service schedule allows you to identify opportunities more easily for upselling or cross-selling. For example, during an annual risk assessment, you might discover that the client's business has expanded

The Ultimate Advantage

overseas, opening a discussion for international coverage options.

Lastly, a well-thought-out schedule of service shows that you are not just interested in selling a policy but are committed to a long-term partnership. It says you are proactive about helping the client manage risks, stay compliant, and grow their business.

In a marketplace where agents often promise the world but deliver much less, a comprehensive schedule of service acts as a tangible commitment to professional, consistent, and value-added service. It becomes a living document of your relationship with the client, constantly evolving but always providing a stable foundation for trust and collaboration.

Tom looked at his calendar and realized it was time for the Initial Onboarding Meeting with Jorge, his new client. Jorge had recently signed a comprehensive insurance policy for his fast-growing manufacturing facility. Tom had been looking forward to this meeting; it was the kickoff for a long-term relationship, and he wanted to make sure everything started on the right foot.

Initial Onboarding Meeting

Tom and his team walked into Jorge's modern, bustling manufacturing facility and were led to a conference room. "Jorge, it's great to see you again," he began. "I've brought Tina and Mark from my service team. Tina will handle your day-to-day account needs, and Mark is our risk analyst."

"Nice to meet you both," Jorge greeted Tina and Mark.

Tom continued, "We're here to go over the policy in detail and set up the software you'll use to manage it. We want to make sure you're fully comfortable with everything from day one."

Thirty-Day Check-in

A month had passed since the onboarding meeting. Tom gave Jorge a call. "Hey, Jorge, just checking in. How has your first month been? Any issues or questions about the policy or software?"

"No, all is good. The system is user-friendly, and the team is comfortable navigating it," Jorge responded.

"Fantastic! If any questions arise, remember Tina is your go-to person," Tom reminded him.

Quarterly Business Reviews

Three months later, Tom visited Jorge's facility. They walked through the plant, and Jorge pointed out a new assembly line. Tom took notes. "This could require a modification in your coverage," Tom said. "I'm glad we caught this early."

Bi-annual Educational Webinars

Jorge received an email invitation to a webinar hosted by Tom's agency. "Managing Risks in Manufacturing," was the title. Jorge found the session enlightening, particularly the section about mitigating risks related to machinery breakdowns.

Pre-renewal Meeting

The Ultimate Advantage

As the policy's renewal date approached, Tom and his service team met with Jorge. "Any changes in your operations? New assets? New risks?" Tom inquired.

"We're planning to expand our product line," Jorge mentioned. Tom nodded, making notes for adjustments in the policy.

Renewal Strategy Session

A month before the renewal, Tom presented several options to Jorge. "Given your expansion, I recommend adding cyber insurance, especially to protect your digital assets and data," Tom suggested.

"That sounds wise," Jorge agreed.

Annual Risk Assessment

Tina and Mark returned to the facility for a full risk assessment, covering everything from worker safety to cybersecurity. "We've come up with some actionable recommendations," Mark reported.

Client Satisfaction Survey

At the end of the year, Jorge received a survey. He rated his experience with Tom's agency highly, particularly praising the proactive risk assessments and educational content.

Client Appreciation Events

One fine day, Jorge received an anniversary celebration card and thoughtful personalized gift from Tom's agency. It was a framed painting featuring gears and sprockets, which would look perfect in his office.

Upselling and Cross-selling: Expanding Coverage as the Client Grows

Cross-selling to an existing book of business isn't just an additional revenue stream for insurance agents; it's an integral part of building long-term relationships based on trust, expertise, and added value. When we talk about cross-selling, the immediate assumption might be that it's just another sales tactic aimed at boosting the bottom line. However, in the world of insurance, particularly when dealing with enterprise-level clients, it's much more than that. It's about understanding your client's business as a whole and offering solutions that help mitigate risks across the board.

Every expansion a business undertakes, every new market they enter, and every new product they launch comes with a unique set of risks. When an insurance agent takes a holistic approach to understand these risks, they become more than just a vendor; they become a valued business consultant. By identifying these potential risks early and offering effective solutions to transfer them, agents provide an indispensable service that can save businesses from disastrous costs in the long run.

Imagine missing the chance to suggest cyber liability insurance to a client who's investing heavily in their digital infrastructure. If a cyber-attack happens, the financial and reputational loss for the client can be staggering. Now consider the potential fallout for you, the insurance agent, who missed the opportunity to mitigate this risk. Not only have you failed in your duty to fully protect your client, but you've also opened the door for other agents to swoop in and present a more comprehensive solution. This is precisely why cross-selling isn't merely about selling; it's about protecting your client's interests and, by extension, your own.

In today's competitive market, clients have an array of choices. If you're not proactive about meeting all of their insurance needs, there's always another agent waiting in the wings eager to offer what you haven't. When another agent gets even a small foothold with one of your clients by providing a type of coverage you haven't offered, it's often only a matter of time before they start encroaching on other areas of your business relationship. Therefore, a failure to cross-sell effectively isn't just a missed opportunity; it's a vulnerability.

Cross-selling also enables a more streamlined approach to managing risks. When a client has multiple policies with the same agent, it's easier to identify gaps in coverage, reduce redundancies, and create a more coordinated response to any issues that arise. This creates not only efficiencies for the client but also strengthens the agent-client relationship, cementing the agent's role as a trusted advisor rather than just a service provider.

Moreover, offering enterprise-wide solutions through effective cross-selling can result in cost savings for the client, as bundling different types of insurance often comes with financial incentives. This adds another layer to the value you provide, making it even less likely that a client will consider alternatives.

Finally, let's talk about data and analytics. The more policies you hold with a client, the better your understanding of their risk profile. This data is invaluable when it comes to

The Ultimate Advantage

tailoring insurance solutions that are not just comprehensive but also cost-effective.

Cross-selling is not a pure sales strategy; it's a customer service strategy. It's a commitment to the client's long-term success and a barrier against competitors who are always looking for an opening. By adopting a holistic approach to risk management, agents can provide enterprise-wide solutions that serve both the client's and their own long-term interests.

Tom's professional ethos as an insurance agent extended beyond merely setting up policies and ensuring timely renewals. He took pride in serving as a trusted advisor to his clients, alerting them to risks they may not even be aware of, and suggesting effective strategies to mitigate those risks. This wasn't just about generating more revenue through upsells or cross-sells; this was about genuinely taking care of the client.

When Tom visited Jorge's facility for the Quarterly Business Review, he took careful note of the expanded assembly lines and additional staff. These changes weren't just signs of Jorge's business success; they were also indicators of new risks.

"As you expand, your operational complexities also increase," Tom pointed out. "Have you considered the risk of cyberattacks now that you have more digital assets and data to protect?"

Jorge shook his head. "Honestly, I've been so focused on the production side that I haven't given that much thought."

This was a typical scenario for many business owners, hyper-focused on growth but not always aware of the accompanying risks. Tom had seen it many times before, and he knew exactly what to recommend.

"I would strongly suggest adding cyber insurance to your policy," Tom advised. "In today's digital age, it's not a matter of if a cyber-attack will happen, but when. Cyber insurance can protect your business assets and client data, offering you peace of mind as you continue to grow."

Jorge looked thoughtful. "That sounds important. Let's add that."

This was what Tom aimed for in his role—helping clients like Jorge foresee risks and providing solutions to manage them. It was about crafting coverage that evolved as the client's business grew, shaping the policy to fit like a second skin, so that the entrepreneur could focus on what they do best: running their business.

In another meeting, Tom noticed that Jorge had started exporting some products. Seizing the moment, he suggested a policy for international liability, covering legal issues that could arise overseas. Jorge agreed, appreciating that Tom was proactive about covering all angles of risk.

By consistently identifying needs and suggesting relevant add-ons, Tom wasn't just upselling or cross-selling policies. He was building a robust, responsive insurance portfolio for Jorge that aimed to protect against the unforeseeable. For Tom, this wasn't just about business; it was about a commitment to his client's well-being, ensuring that as risks emerged, they were immediately met with effective strategies for mitigation.

Through these actions, Tom demonstrated that insurance wasn't a one-size-fits-all product to be sold and forgotten. It was a dynamic relationship, changing as the client's business changed. And by doing so, Tom wasn't just an insurance agent to Jorge; he was a partner in the truest sense of the word, deeply invested in the long-term success and safety of Jorge's enterprise.

When you find yourself working in an agency that doesn't have a standard service schedule or isn't aligned with a more holistic and comprehensive approach to client relationships, it can be frustrating. But rather than resigning yourself to the status quo or looking for greener pastures, there are constructive steps you can take to bring about meaningful change from within.

First, it might be beneficial to give a copy of this book (Shameless Plug) to the agency's management and mention the section that outlines these best practices. Words on a page from a third-party source can often validate your concerns and solutions in a way that a simple conversation might not. Remember, books like this one that advocate for a structured, client-centered approach to insurance sales and service aren't like the average business book; they're a guide to a more successful and ethical way of doing business. A good leader will recognize and appreciate the initiative and the opportunity for improvement.

Now, let's talk about the real meat of the matter: implementing these practices when your agency doesn't currently have a standard service schedule. Understand that even though implementing a structured service schedule is not inherently difficult, the challenge lies in disrupting established workflows and dealing with resistance to change. But with a bit of strategic planning and effective communication, you can make it work.

Begin by collaborating with your account managers. They are the ones who will help you operationalize this new approach. Schedule a series of meetings to map out a plan, outlining each milestone along the way. This could range from implementing a thirty-day check-in with clients to arranging quarterly business reviews. Importantly, your account managers can help ensure that your new approach doesn't just sound good on paper but is genuinely practicable.

Next, it's time to bring in the agency principal. Any significant change in client servicing strategy needs to have the buy-in from the top. Make your case compelling by showing how this new approach will not only improve client retention but will also enhance the agency's reputation and bottom line. Discuss the potential for cross-selling and illustrate how that increases the lifetime value of each client. And remember to bring up how these changes can make the agency more competitive, turning it into a market leader rather than a follower.

Now, if you're concerned about the administrative workload these new initiatives might add, consider employing technology. Various tools can automate client outreach, schedule check-ins, and even analyze customer data to identify cross-selling opportunities. This isn't about adding to your workload; it's about working smarter.

It's essential to set up metrics for success. Discuss with your team what success looks like and how it will be measured. Maybe it's a higher Net Promoter Score, increased client retention, or additional policies per client. Whatever your key performance indicators are, make sure everyone is aware and on board.

Now, let's address the potential objection that many of these practices are "nice-to-haves" but not essential. In the highly competitive world of insurance sales, the difference between a "nice-to-have" and a "must-have" often boils down to the difference between a lost client and a retained one. What seems optional in good times becomes critical in challenging ones. Make sure your agency understands that this is about long-term sustainability.

Finally, always keep lines of communication open. This is new for everyone, and there will inevitably be hiccups along the way. Make it clear that feedback is not just welcome but actively encouraged. Only through ongoing conversation can the approach be refined and optimized.

In summary, while working in an agency without a set service schedule or a holistic client approach can be challenging, it also presents a significant opportunity for growth and improvement. And who better to lead that change than you, a producer committed to not just meeting but exceeding client expectations? With strategic planning, teamwork, and a little bit of courage, you can transform your agency for the better.

Identify Needs: As the client's business expands, so will their risk. Identify gaps in their current coverage.

Suggest Relevant Add-Ons: Recommend additional policies or coverage that cater to their evolving needs.

Chapter 9: Time Management & Productivity Hacks

The Essential Time Management Guide for Insurance Producers

The role of an insurance producer involves juggling various responsibilities, from client meetings to back-end administrative work. Mastering the art of time management can drastically improve your efficiency and success rate. This guide will delve into the significance of time blocking and guarding your time for various activities.

Time Blocking

Essentially, this involves dedicating chunks of time to a specific task or set of tasks. This method allows you to bring structure to your day and minimizes the time lost in switching between different activities. For example, designate the first two hours of your workday for client follow-ups and the last two for preparing presentations or paperwork.

The insurance industry is teeming with tasks that range from prospecting and client meetings to policy reviews and endless paperwork. In such a busy environment, how can you manage your time most effectively to achieve optimal results? The answer lies in the disciplined practice of time blocking.

The Basics of Time Blocking

Time blocking is more than just a time management tool; it's a strategy that enables you to perform at your best. By dividing your day into specific, predefined periods (or "blocks") allocated to certain tasks, you give yourself the framework to work more productively. You bring order to the chaos by making an advanced commitment to a particular course of action during a designated time slot.

The Benefits of Time Blocking

Time blocking provides structure to your otherwise erratic workdays, enhancing focus and reducing procrastination. With less idle time and fewer opportunities to succumb to distractions, you can deepen your work and produce higher-quality results.

Minimizing Context Switching

Time lost to switching between different activities can be substantial. The mental effort required to cease one task and gear up for another can diminish your productivity and cognitive function over time. By using time blocking to

The Ultimate Advantage

group similar activities, you cut down on the costs of context switching, preserving your mental resources for more significant challenges.

How to Implement Time Blocking

Plan: Ideally, your time blocks should be set up in advance—whether it's the night before or a week ahead. This way, you know exactly what's on the agenda when you start your day.

Use Tools: Utilize calendars, apps, or old-fashioned paper to chart out your time blocks. Google Calendar or specialized time-blocking apps can be particularly effective for setting reminders and adjusting plans on the fly.

Be Realistic: While it's tempting to block out every minute of the day, it's crucial to leave gaps for unexpected tasks, emergencies, or simply to catch your breath.

Review and Revise: At the end of the week, take some time to assess how well your time blocks worked and adjust for the following week. Did you allocate too much or too little time for certain tasks? Were there unexpected interruptions that consistently threw off your plan? Use this feedback to refine your time blocks for the next week.

Specialized Time Blocks for Insurance Producers

Insurance producers may find it helpful to create specific categories for their time blocks, such as:

Client Interaction: Allocate specific hours for calling, emailing, or meeting with clients.

Prospecting: Set aside time for identifying and reaching out to potential clients.

Policy Review and Paperwork: Create blocks specifically for policy reviews, documentation, and other forms of paperwork.

Training and Development: Reserve time for self-improvement, whether that's studying industry trends, taking courses, or attending webinars.

Administrative Tasks: Don't forget to block out time for the nitty-gritty back-end work that keeps the wheels turning, like data entry or scheduling.

Guarding Your Time Blocks

Your time blocks are a commitment to yourself and your productivity, so guard them fiercely. Make it known among your team and clients that these are periods when you'll be focusing on specific tasks and will not be available for impromptu meetings or distractions.

By mastering the art of time blocking, you can manage your tasks, minimize wasted time, and focus on what truly matters in your role as an insurance producer. This structured approach sets you up not just for a more productive workday, but for a more fulfilling and successful career.

When we talk about guarding time, we mean being selective and intentional about what you agree to do. Not every meeting request or task needs to be accepted immediately. Consider the value and urgency of each request before slotting it into your calendar.

Top Ten Productivity Hacks

1. The Eisenhower Box Technique: A Roadmap for Prioritizing Tasks

Success in any industry, especially one as demanding as insurance, hinges on your ability to prioritize effectively. While time management is crucial, knowing what to manage within those blocks of time is equally important. Enter the Eisenhower Box technique, a simple yet transformative tool to segregate tasks based on their urgency and importance.

The Essence of the Eisenhower Box Technique

The Eisenhower Box, also known as the Urgent-Important Matrix, is a four-quadrant box that serves as a classification system for your to-dos. The horizontal axis represents urgency, and the vertical axis indicates importance. This creates four categories:

Urgent and Important: Tasks that must be done immediately, such as meeting client deadlines or handling crises.

Important, Not Urgent: Activities that contribute to long-term benefits but don't need immediate attention, such as strategic planning or relationship building.

Urgent, Not Important: Tasks that demand your attention now but don't contribute to long-term goals. These could be interruptions or certain types of emails.

Neither Urgent Nor Important: Activities that don't contribute to your goals and don't need immediate attention, like aimless web browsing.

Practical Implementation for Insurance Producers

As an insurance producer, your urgent and important tasks might include responding to client emergencies, meeting regulatory deadlines, or resolving discrepancies in policies. These tasks require immediate attention and often can't be delegated or postponed. Block off time specifically for these high-priority activities, so you're not scrambling at the last minute.

Tasks that are important but not urgent could include professional development, networking, or long-term strategic planning for client acquisition. These tasks are vital for career growth but lack pressing deadlines. Reserve dedicated blocks in your weekly or monthly schedule for these activities.

Urgent but not important tasks often appear as interruptions, like unscheduled calls or minor queries from team members. While these tasks seem to demand immediate attention, they often can be deferred, delegated, or even declined. Use the "touch it once" principle here; make an instant decision on whether the task is worth your time.

Lastly, tasks that are neither urgent nor important should be eliminated or minimized as much as possible. These time-wasters detract from your ability to focus on truly impactful activities. Identify these tasks and make a conscious effort to avoid them.

The Value of Prioritization

The Eisenhower Box is not just a task management tool, it's a method for value assessment. It compels you to consider the long-term impact of your daily activities, guiding you toward tasks that are aligned with your goals and values. For an insurance producer, this prioritization is invaluable for balancing the often-conflicting demands of client relationships, sales targets, administrative work, and personal development.

The Eisenhower Box technique offers a straightforward yet effective way to manage the ever-changing landscape of responsibilities that come with being an insurance producer. By routinely classifying tasks based on their urgency and importance, you set the stage for both immediate effectiveness and long-term success. So the next time you're drowning in a sea of tasks, take a moment to draw your Eisenhower Box. You'll find that it not only brings

The Ultimate Advantage

clarity but also introduces a transformative shift in how you approach your work.

2. The Art of Batch Processing: A Key to Efficiency and Reduced Mental Load

In today's fast-paced work environment, multi-tasking seems like a necessary evil. However, continually switching between tasks is not only counterproductive but also mentally exhausting. For professionals, especially insurance producers juggling a plethora of responsibilities—client meetings, administrative work, networking, and more—a more efficient approach is needed. This is where the concept of batch processing comes into play.

What Is Batch Processing?

Batch processing is a time-management strategy that involves grouping similar tasks together and tackling them in a single time block. Instead of sporadically responding to emails throughout the day, for instance, you might dedicate one hour solely to this activity. The idea is to minimize the cognitive load that comes with task-switching by remaining in the same "mental zone" for a specific time

Why Batch Processing Is Effective

Reduced Mental Fatigue: Continuously shifting your focus between unrelated tasks depletes your mental energy. Batch processing mitigates this by keeping your brain engaged in a similar type of activity for a set period.

Improved Concentration: When you're not constantly distracted by the need to change gears, you can delve deeper into the task at hand. This level of focus usually leads to higher quality work.

Time-Saving: Each time you switch tasks, there's a "ramp-up" time as your brain adjusts to the new activity. Batching eliminates multiple ramp-up periods, saving valuable minutes—or even hours—over the course of a day.

Practical Applications for Insurance Producers

In the world of insurance sales, there are myriad tasks that can benefit from batch processing.

Client Communication: Instead of responding to emails or messages as they come in, allocate specific time blocks for correspondence. This will enable you to complete thoughtful replies without being perpetually interrupted.

Policy Review: Whether it's going through the finer details of policies or comparing different plans, these tasks require deep focus. Reserve a block of time where you can immerse yourself in this activity without distractions.

Administrative Work: Tasks like invoicing, filing, and updating records are often put off but are essential for smooth operations. Batch these together and tackle them in one go to ensure nothing falls through the cracks.

Prospect Research: Identifying potential clients is another area where batch processing can be a boon. By dedicating a block of time to this, you can streamline your outreach efforts more effectively.

The Balanced Approach

While batch processing is highly effective, it's crucial to balance it with other time management strategies. For instance, urgent tasks will inevitably crop up and will need immediate attention, regardless of your batch processing schedule. The key is to find a balanced approach that combines batching with a level of flexibility.

Batch processing isn't just about clubbing similar tasks together; it's about creating an environment where your mind can operate at its peak efficiency. For insurance

The Ultimate Advantage

producers, whose roles demand both breadth and depth of focus, embracing batch processing can be a game-changer. It streamlines workflow, reduces mental load, and ultimately, allows for the delivery of more effective and timely service to clients.

3. Mastering the Pomodoro Technique: The Secret to Productive Focus

In an era characterized by endless distractions and constant demands on our attention, achieving sustained focus has become an uphill battle. For professionals in demanding fields like insurance, where producers must juggle client interactions, policy evaluations, and administrative duties, finding a productivity method that really works is crucial. This is where the Pomodoro Technique comes into play, offering a balanced approach to manage time and focus effectively.

What Is the Pomodoro Technique?

The Pomodoro Technique is a time management system that encourages people to work within the bounds of their attention span—typically around twenty-five minutes at a time, followed by a short, rejuvenating break. These intervals are called "Pomodoros," named after the tomato-shaped kitchen timer that was originally used by the technique's founder, Francesco Cirillo.

The Basic Framework

The basic premise is deceptively simple but incredibly effective:

1. Choose a task or set of tasks you want to work on.
2. Set a timer for twenty-five minutes.
3. Work on the task until the timer rings.
4. Take a five-minute break.

5. Repeat.

   After completing four Pomodoros, take a longer break of around fifteen to thirty minutes to recharge.

   Why It Works

   Attention Management: The Pomodoro Technique dovetails neatly with how our brains are wired. Humans can only focus intensely for a short period before their attention starts to wane. Working in short bursts ensures you are operating at peak efficiency.

   Counteracts Procrastination: Knowing you only have to work for twenty-five minutes makes even daunting tasks seem more manageable, reducing the temptation to procrastinate.

   Encourages Regular Rest: The scheduled breaks ensure you step away from your work, reducing the risk of burnout and mental fatigue.

   Provides Structure: The Pomodoro Technique brings structure to your workday, helping you allocate finite blocks of time to tasks, which in turn helps in setting realistic goals and expectations.

   Practical Application for Insurance Producers

   For insurance producers, the Pomodoro Technique can be particularly beneficial for a number of key tasks:

   Client Follow-Ups: Allocate a couple of Pomodoros in the morning for client follow-ups. Knowing you have a limited time makes the process efficient and focused.

   Policy Reviews: These require concentration and attention to detail. A Pomodoro or two can be beneficial to go through policy documents carefully without getting lost in the labyrinth of legal jargon.

Administrative Duties: Even paperwork can become less of a chore when tackled in Pomodoros. The sense of urgency keeps you on track and may even make these mundane tasks somewhat enjoyable.

Research and Development: Whether you're looking into new insurance policies or studying market trends, the Pomodoro Technique can help you delve deeper into subjects without feeling overwhelmed.

Team Meetings: While it's unconventional, applying the Pomodoro Technique to meetings can make them more focused and efficient. Knowing there's a finite amount of time keeps everyone on task.

Flexibility within Discipline

It's worth noting that the Pomodoro Technique isn't rigid. Feel free to adjust the lengths of both the work and break periods according to what suits you best. Some people find that fifty-minute work intervals with ten-minute breaks are more conducive to their workflow.

The Pomodoro Technique offers a perfect blend of discipline and flexibility. It's not just about working hard but also about working smart. For insurance producers tasked with a multitude of responsibilities, it provides a balanced, sustainable way to manage one's time and attention. In a world where focus is a dwindling resource, mastering the Pomodoro Technique could be your ticket to unprecedented productivity and success.

4. The Art of Limiting Distractions: Cultivating Focus in a Distracted World

In today's hyper-connected world, distractions are just a fingertip away. Notifications from social media, endless pings from group chats, and the constant influx of emails are just a few examples. For insurance producers, who are often juggling client interactions, administrative tasks, and team coordination, minimizing distractions is not just an ideal—it's a necessity. The ability to focus without interruptions directly correlates with productivity and, ultimately, success.

The "Do Not Disturb" Function

A simple but effective tool for achieving a distraction-free environment is the "Do Not Disturb" function found on most smartphones and computers. Activating this mode silences all notifications, calls, and alerts, allowing you to work with unwavering concentration. This feature is especially useful when you're performing tasks that require intense focus, such as reviewing complex policy documents, preparing for client meetings, or strategizing for account renewals.

Why Limiting Distractions Matters

Enhanced Productivity: The more focused you are, the faster and more efficiently you can complete tasks. Every interruption disrupts your flow, making tasks take longer than they should.

Improved Quality of Work: Distractions can lead to errors, and in the insurance industry, even a minor oversight can have significant consequences. Limiting distractions allows you to work with greater accuracy.

Mental Well-Being: Constant interruptions create stress by breaking your flow and forcing your brain to switch gears frequently. A more focused work environment contributes to mental well-being, reducing stress and boosting job satisfaction.

Tools and Techniques Beyond "Do Not Disturb"

While the "Do Not Disturb" function is a great start, several other methods can help you create a distraction-free work environment:

Physical Barriers: Sometimes it's as simple as closing your office door to signify to coworkers that you're in a focus period and should not be interrupted.

Time-Blocking: Allocate specific time blocks for focused work and make it known that you are not to be disturbed during these times. This can be communicated through team calendars or even a simple note at your workspace.

Web Blockers: Browser extensions that limit your access to distracting websites can also be incredibly useful. You can set them to be active during your focus periods, ensuring you aren't tempted to take a "quick look" at social media or news sites.

Prioritize Tasks: Create a to-do list that separates tasks by urgency and importance, so that you can devote your undistracted time to what truly matters.

Commitment to Focus

Limiting distractions is not a one-time effort but a consistent practice. It involves cultivating a work environment—both physically and digitally—that is conducive to concentration. This may require conversations with your team about respecting focus periods or setting up guidelines about when and how it's appropriate to approach you with urgent matters.

In the fast-paced world of insurance, where responsiveness is often key, balancing accessibility with the need for focus can be a challenge. But mastering this balance through limiting distractions will significantly improve not only your work output but also the quality of your professional life.

5. The Power of Automation: A Super Power for Insurance Producers

The life of an insurance producer is replete with a mix of client-facing activities, administrative work, and strategic planning. Amid this whirlwind of duties, even the most skilled producers find themselves bogged down with mundane tasks such as data entry and appointment scheduling. These repetitive responsibilities can consume an inordinate amount of time that could be better spent on high-value activities like client acquisition or portfolio management. The solution to this time conundrum lies in one word: Automation.

Why Automation Is Critical

Efficiency and Accuracy: Automation software reduces the room for human error, which is often inevitable when one is engaged in monotonous tasks. A simple typo can lead to miscommunication or even financial loss. Automation software ensures that such minutiae are handled precisely every time, freeing you from having to double-check every entry.

Time-Saving: Automation allows you to delegate repetitive tasks to a system that can perform them in a fraction of the time it would take a human. This time-saving aspect is particularly crucial for producers, who often work in highly competitive environments where every minute counts.

Scalability: As your client base grows, the administrative demands will grow proportionally. Automation tools scale with your business, making them a sustainable long-term solution.

Common Tasks to Automate

The Ultimate Advantage

Data Entry: CRM software can be programmed to automatically update client profiles, transaction histories, and policy details. Some platforms even sync with other business software, so you don't have to manually enter the same information in multiple places.

Appointment Scheduling: Automating this can be as simple as setting up an online calendar where clients can book, reschedule, or cancel their appointments, which then automatically syncs with your personal calendar. Reminder emails or text messages can be sent out automatically as the appointment date approaches.

Client Follow-Ups: Automated email sequences can be programmed to go out at specific times or based on certain triggers, like a client inquiry or policy renewal date, ensuring consistent communication.

Choosing the Right Automation Tools

The market is filled with a plethora of software solutions designed to automate various aspects of business operations. When selecting a tool, consider factors like ease of use, scalability, and how well it integrates with your existing systems. A bit of research and perhaps some free trials will help you make an informed decision.

A Commitment to Continuous Improvement

It's important to regularly assess the effectiveness of your automated processes. Are they saving you as much time as you had hoped? Are there any glitches that need to be addressed? This should be a continuous process aimed at maximizing efficiency.

Automation does more than just simplify your life; it fundamentally transforms how you operate, enabling you to devote more time to what really matters: building relationships and growing your client base. By automating repetitive tasks, you're not just working smarter; you're also offering a more streamlined, efficient service that will impress and retain clients.

6. The Art of Delegation: Empowering Your Team to Drive Success

As a producer in the insurance industry, your expertise and skill set are critical for generating new business, nurturing client relationships, and overseeing essential strategy shifts. However, no matter how talented you are, you're still limited by the number of hours in a day. One of the most effective ways to optimize your time and resources is through the skillful art of delegation.

The Importance of Delegation

Frees up Time for Revenue-Generating Activities: By entrusting routine or technical tasks to team members, you can free up your schedule to focus on high-impact activities like meeting prospective clients or developing new products.

Increases Team Efficiency and Skills: Delegating empowers your team to develop new skills and expertise. Not only does this increase the overall capacity of your team, but it also enhances job satisfaction among team members, which can lead to higher retention rates.

Optimizes Skill Allocation: Every individual on your team has unique skills and talents. Delegation allows for the better allocation of tasks based on each person's abilities, which leads to more efficient and effective outcomes.

What Can Be Delegated

Administrative Duties: Tasks like data entry, appointment scheduling, and initial client follow-ups are important but don't require your specialized skill set. These can be easily delegated to administrative staff or customer service representatives.

Market Research: While it's essential to understand market trends and customer needs, the actual process of collecting and analyzing this data can be handed off to a skilled analyst within your team.

Initial Client Qualification: Screening potential clients can be delegated to a sales team who can then pass on qualified leads to you for further nurturing and closing.

Effective Delegation Strategies

Set Clear Objectives and Expectations: When delegating a task, ensure that the team member understands the desired outcome, the deadline, and any relevant processes or guidelines.

Choose the Right Person: Delegate tasks to team members who have the appropriate skill sets, experience, or interest in the task at hand.

Follow Up and Feedback: After delegation, it's crucial to have a mechanism for follow-up and feedback. This enables you to make sure the task is on track to be completed as required and allows for adjustments as needed.

Be Open to Reverse Delegation: Sometimes team members might try to push tasks back onto you. Be clear that once a task is delegated, you expect it to be completed by the assignee, barring any significant challenges that truly require your attention.

Concluding Thoughts

Delegation isn't just about offloading tasks to others it's about building a more resilient, capable, and efficient team. As you foster a culture of trust and empower team members to take on more responsibilities, you'll find that your own time is freed up to drive strategic initiatives, innovate, and deliver exceptional service to your clients. The ability to effectively delegate is a hallmark of a great leader and a successful producer.

7. The Power of an Organized Workspace: Boosting Productivity for Insurance Producers

The impact of your workspace on productivity and mental clarity is often underestimated. Whether you're operating from a traditional office or a remote workspace maintaining an organized workspace is essential for success, particularly for insurance producers whose day-to-day activities involve juggling multiple tasks and responsibilities as well as building relationships.

Psychological Benefits

Enhanced Focus: Clutter is a visual distraction. When your eyes move around a cluttered space, your brain has more stimuli to process, which can decrease your cognitive resources for other tasks. An organized workspace, devoid of unnecessary clutter, allows your brain to focus entirely on the task at hand.

Reduced Stress: A cluttered workspace can make you feel overwhelmed, activating stress responses that can adversely affect decision-making and problem-solving abilities. By maintaining an organized workspace, you send a positive signal to your brain, reducing feelings of stress and anxiety.

Efficiency and Time Management

Streamlined Workflow: Knowing where everything is can significantly speed up your daily operations. Whether it's essential documents, digital files, or even stationery, an organized workspace ensures you don't waste precious minutes—or even hours—looking for things.

Clear Separation of Tasks: Use dedicated areas or organizers for different tasks or types of work. This could be as simple as having separate trays for pending and completed paperwork, or more complex, like designated zones in your office for client meetings, research, and administrative work.

Professionalism and Client Perceptions

First Impressions Matter: When meeting clients, especially high-profile ones, a clean and organized office can give an excellent first impression. Your workspace reflects your professional attitude and can subtly indicate to clients that you are competent, organized, and reliable.

Confidentiality: For insurance producers, maintaining client confidentiality is not just ethical but often legally required.

An organized workspace ensures that sensitive documents are appropriately filed and secured, away from prying eyes.

Personalization and Mental Well-Being

Personal Touch: While keeping your workspace organized is essential, don't forget to make it "yours." Photos, plants, or anything else that brings you joy can be part of your workspace, elevating your mood and allowing more of your own personality to shine through.

Flexibility: An organized workspace allows for greater flexibility. If you need to switch gears quickly—from a client, call to drafting a complex proposal—an organized workspace ensures that you can do so without additional stress or time delays.

For an insurance producer, time is often equivalent to money. The benefits of an organized workspace are multifold, from psychological advantages like enhanced focus and reduced stress to practical aspects like streamlined workflow and better time management. Even the impression it leaves on clients can be a game-changer in a competitive market. Therefore, investing some time and effort into organizing your workspace can result in a significant payoff in productivity, efficiency, and overall well-being.

8. Conducting a Time Audit

For insurance producers who often find themselves swamped with tasks like client meetings, paperwork, and administrative duties, time is an invaluable resource. Managing this time effectively becomes a vital part of achieving both short-term and long-term goals. One of the most efficient ways to improve your efficiency and time management skills is by performing a time audit. Here's why you should do it and how.

Why a Time Audit?

Identify Time Drains: Many times, we aren't even aware of how our time is being spent, leading to inefficiencies that could otherwise be avoided. A time audit provides a clear picture of your activities and the time spent on them, allowing you to identify and cut out tasks that don't align with your goals.

Resource Allocation: It provides an overview of how much time is being allocated to high-priority tasks as opposed to lower-priority activities. This can be crucial in an industry like insurance where time-sensitive actions can significantly impact the business.

Improves Focus and Productivity: Knowing exactly where your time goes can help you adjust your focus and direct it towards activities that are both urgent and important, thus improving your overall productivity.

How to Conduct a Time Audit

Logging Your Time: For a week, keep a detailed record of your activities. Use a digital tool or a simple notepad to jot down tasks and the time spent on them. The granularity of the log will depend on how detailed you want your audit to be; some find it helpful to log every fifteen minutes.

Categorization: At the end of the week, categorize these tasks. How many client meetings did you have and how much time did each one take? How much time was spent on admin work? How long did you spend composing and responding to emails?

Analysis: Look for patterns and time drains. Are there tasks that took up a disproportionate amount of time but aren't considered urgent or important? How much time did you spend on revenue-generating activities?

Prioritization: Based on this analysis, prioritize your activities. What needs more of your attention? What can be delegated or done more efficiently?

Action Plan: Create an action plan to redirect your time towards activities that are directly aligned with your business objectives. This could mean automating certain tasks, delegating others, or simply eliminating activities that do not add value.

Impact on Business Growth

Insurance is a highly competitive sector where even a small mistake can cost you a client. Effective time management can be your key differentiator, and a time audit is a simple yet powerful tool to achieve that.

In the race against time, having a thorough understanding of your time expenditure can provide you with the upper hand. It can offer actionable insights into improving your workflow, streamlining tasks, and ultimately, providing a higher quality of service to your clients. A time audit isn't just a task you do once and forget; it's a continuous improvement.

9.SMART Goals: The Foundation for all Success

For insurance agents striving to excel in their careers, setting goals is not just beneficial; it's essential. However, simply having goals is not enough. Your objectives must be clear, precise, and actionable to propel you toward success. This is where the SMART goals framework comes into play. SMART stands for Specific, Measurable, Achievable, Relevant, and Time-bound. Applying this methodology can

The Ultimate Advantage

make a tremendous difference in your effectiveness as an agent and your ability to meet and exceed targets.

Specificity Is Key

General goals are almost like wishes—they're vague and give you nothing concrete to work toward. Instead of saying, "I want to increase my sales," a SMART goal would be, "I want to increase sales of life insurance policies by 10% this quarter." Specificity pinpoints what needs to be achieved, thereby making the goal actionable.

Making Goals Measurable

If you can't measure it, you can't manage it. Having a measurable target allows you to track your progress and understand how close you are to achieving your goal. Measurable goals have metrics: numbers, percentages, or any form of quantifiable benchmark. For example, instead of saying, "I want to get more clients," say, "I want to acquire five new clients each month." This gives you a clear metric to evaluate your progress against.

Setting Achievable Goals

As an insurance agent, you should set goals that stretch you but are still within reach given your resources, knowledge, and time. Setting goals that are too high will only set you up for failure, leading to discouragement and decreased motivation. At the same time, goals that are too easy won't drive you to excel. The key is to find the balance by setting objectives that are challenging yet achievable.

Relevance to the Bigger Picture

Every goal you set should be relevant to your long-term career objectives or the objectives of your agency. Ask yourself how this goal aligns with the broader company strategy or your own professional development. Is this the right time for this goal? Do you have the resources and skills to make this happen now? Relevance ensures you're not wasting time on objectives that don't move you closer to your ultimate aims.

Time-Bound for Urgency

Every goal needs a timeline. Deadlines create urgency and keep you focused. Without a time constraint, there's less pressure to take the actions required to meet your objectives. Whether it's a daily, weekly, or monthly target, having a specific date to work toward keeps you disciplined and adds a level of accountability that can be incredibly motivating.

Incorporating SMART goals into your planning as an insurance agent offers a structured and disciplined approach that can greatly impact your performance. It leads you to quantify your ambitions, giving you clear metrics and deadlines that will help you measure your success or lack thereof. It's not just about making a sale today; it's about building a sustainable, rewarding career for the long run. And for that, SMART goal setting provides the most solid foundation you can have.

10. Leveraging Accountability to Elevate Productivity

The notion of accountability is often underestimated in professional settings, especially in roles like that of an insurance producer where individual performance is paramount. However, the power of being accountable to someone other than oneself can act as a catalyst for remarkable growth and productivity. In a role that involves multiple responsibilities, from client meetings to underwriting and claim management, maintaining focus can sometimes be challenging. That's where accountability comes into play.

Choosing the Right Accountability Partner

The first step in this journey is identifying a suitable accountability partner. It could be a colleague, a supervisor, or even a mentor from outside your organization. The critical factor is that this person should be someone you respect and don't want to disappoint. They should also be familiar enough with your line of work to understand your challenges and objectives.

Setting Clear Objectives

Accountability is most effective when there are clear objectives against which to measure performance. These goals should align with your role's requirements and ideally be set using SMART criteria (Specific, Measurable, Achievable, Relevant, Time-bound). Once you have your objectives outlined, share them with your accountability partner. The act of vocalizing your goals makes them more tangible and sets the stage for you to be held accountable for achieving them.

Regular Check-Ins

Consistency is key in any accountability relationship. Establish a regular check-in schedule with your accountability partner. These can be quick, fifteen-minute catch-up sessions once a week to review what you've accomplished and what you're struggling with. Regularity ensures that you're continuously reminded of your responsibilities and deadlines, thereby encouraging you to prioritize more effectively and remain focused.

Honesty and Transparency

It's crucial to be honest and transparent with your accountability partner. If you've missed a target or are finding a particular task challenging, communicate this openly. Honesty invites solutions and constructive feedback, whereas hiding your struggles can create more obstacles. The whole point of accountability is to bring issues into the open where they can be tackled effectively.

Reaping the Rewards

The benefits of this system extend beyond achieving immediate targets. Being accountable for your actions cultivates a heightened sense of responsibility and discipline that will serve you well in your career. It can also contribute to stronger professional relationships and networking opportunities. Moreover, your partner can offer a valuable external perspective, challenging you in ways you hadn't considered and thereby driving your growth as an insurance producer.

Establishing an accountability system is not merely an exercise in scrutiny; it's an empowering strategy to enhance your productivity and work ethic. It's a structured approach to staying on top of tasks, receiving constructive feedback, and continually moving toward your objectives. For insurance producers juggling various responsibilities, it can be the missing link between intention and accomplishment.

Bonus: Prioritizing Activities for Optimal Productivity

In the fast-paced world of insurance, where every minute counts, effective prioritization can make the difference between hitting your targets and falling short. For insurance producers, time management is not a luxury—it's a necessity. Given that you're navigating a landscape filled with client meetings, underwriting evaluations, renewals,

The Ultimate Advantage

and countless other tasks, knowing what to tackle first is crucial. But prioritization isn't just about what appears urgent; it's about recognizing what is genuinely important and aligning that with your core business goals. Here's a detailed look at how you can fine-tune your prioritization skills.

Focus on Value

In the high-stakes world of insurance production, prioritizing tasks that offer the most value is paramount to your success. Value-driven tasks are those that align closely with both your short-term goals and long-term vision for your career or business. Instead of constantly reacting to client queries, it's crucial to allocate designated times for activities that will truly propel you forward.

Setting criteria to measure the "value" of different tasks—whether financial or strategic—enables you to separate what is urgent from what is important. This approach ensures that you don't just navigate through the maze of daily responsibilities but actively build toward more significant, long-term objectives.

By consistently focusing on tasks that offer substantive returns, you'll find that your actions take on an enhanced level of purpose and direction. You'll move from merely surviving the daily grind to proactively shaping your career and contributing to your business growth.

Understand Deadlines

The concept of deadlines in the insurance industry can be complex. Some are hard deadlines that cannot be moved, like policy renewal dates, while others might be more flexible. Knowing these deadlines and planning around them is vital. Create a timeline for each task and work your way through them in a sequence that prevents last-minute rushes, which are often prone to errors. Understanding the temporal aspect of your obligations allows you to allocate resources more wisely, ensuring that you're not just working fast, but also working smart.

Client Importance

In the insurance world, not all clients are created equal, at least not in terms of their immediate impact on your business. Some clients may be lower value in premiums but high in referral potential, while others might be significant accounts that require constant nurturing. The trick is to categorize your clients based on parameters like premium size, referral potential, and strategic fit. This segmentation allows you to allocate time efficiently when balancing multiple clients and tasks. However, remember that while high-value clients may require immediate attention, nurturing smaller clients for long-term growth is also essential.

The Intertwining of Time and Task Management

Effective prioritization is not a standalone skill, it's an integral part of a broader time management strategy. It should be incorporated into daily practices, weekly plans, and even quarterly objectives. That's where techniques like time blocking can be especially useful. By assigning specific "blocks" of time to high-priority tasks, you reduce the temptation to multitask and increase your chance of being able to dive deeper into critical activities.

Review and Adjust

The business landscape can change rapidly, and your priorities today might not be your priorities tomorrow. Hence, it's vital to frequently review and, if necessary, adjust your task list. Use metrics, feedback, and outcomes to evaluate the effectiveness of your prioritization strategy and make data-driven adjustments.

The Ultimate Advantage

The Larger Picture

The real benefit of effective prioritization goes beyond checking off items on a to-do list. It enables you to be in control rather than feeling overwhelmed. It cultivates a sense of purpose in your work, strengthening your commitment to your career and enhancing your job satisfaction.

In summary, by integrating these prioritization principles into your workflow, you can navigate your multifaceted role as an insurance producer with precision and effectiveness. This is not merely about survival but about thriving in an industry that rewards those who can master the art of allocating their time wisely.

Utilizing CRM (Customer Relationship Management) Tools

Streamline Processes: CRMs can automate follow-ups, reminders, and client communication.

Data Analysis: Utilize CRM analytics to identify sales trends, successful strategies, and areas of improvement.

Chapter 10: Continuous Learning and Industry Adaptation

Stay Ahead of the Curve

In an industry as dynamic and complex as this, standing still is tantamount to moving backward. The market is perpetually influenced by a multitude of variables—from regulatory changes and technological advances to shifts in consumer behavior and global economic trends. As a commercial insurance producer, your worth is intrinsically tied to how well you adapt to this fluid landscape. You are

The Ultimate Advantage

not just selling policies; you're selling expertise, trust, and, most importantly, peace of mind. Therefore, a commitment to continuous learning is not a luxury; it's an absolute necessity.

It's tempting to rest on one's laurels, especially after achieving a modicum of success. However, your clients are not static—their businesses grow, technologies change, and risk profiles evolve. What was effective last year or even last quarter may not necessarily apply today. Continuous learning enables you to anticipate these changes and advise clients proactively, reinforcing your role as an indispensable partner rather than just a service provider. By keeping yourself updated, you can offer insights that may save your clients significant amounts of money and, perhaps more importantly, keep them better protected against emerging risks.

One practical way to stay ahead is to engage in industry seminars and workshops regularly. These gatherings provide invaluable insights into market trends and innovative products. Similarly, webinars and online courses offer flexibility for busy schedules. A commercial insurance producer who dedicates time to professional development is better prepared to serve the nuanced needs of their clientele. Further, obtaining additional certifications can give you an edge, bolstering your credibility and deepening your understanding of specialized areas within the insurance ecosystem.

Networking should also be part of your learning strategy. Interactions with peers, mentors, and even competitors can offer fresh perspectives and may alert you to trends or opportunities you hadn't considered. A casual conversation at an industry event can sometimes yield a nugget of wisdom worth its weight in gold.

Another dimension of continuous learning is client feedback. Make it a practice to solicit opinions about your service, ideally through formal mechanisms like client satisfaction surveys or post-project reviews. This feedback can serve as an invaluable learning tool, providing actionable insights that you can apply to future engagements.

Technology, too, is an area where continuous learning can pay dividends. Insurance tech is evolving at a rapid clip, offering tools that can significantly enhance efficiency, from client relationship management software to complex risk assessment algorithms. Learning how to leverage these tools can provide you with a significant competitive advantage.

Then there's the legislative aspect. Insurance laws and regulations are ever-changing landscapes that can greatly impact your work and your advice to clients. A keen understanding of current and upcoming laws, including how they will affect different industries you serve, is vital for your credibility and effectiveness.

Remember, in this industry, your most potent asset is your knowledge. Clients are not just buying a policy; they are buying expertise and assurance. The more you know, the more valuable you become. Your worth as a commercial insurance producer is amplified exponentially by your willingness to continually learn and adapt.

Continuous learning is the cornerstone upon which a successful career in commercial insurance is built. The landscape will continue to evolve, propelled by technological innovation, changing regulations, and shifts in the global economy. By committing to continuous learning and adaptation, you're not just surviving these changes; you're capitalizing on them. You're converting challenges

The Ultimate Advantage

into opportunities and, in the process, proving your invaluable worth to your clients, today and into the future.

Staying Updated: Market Trends, Policy Changes, and New Products

In the fast-paced, ever-changing world of commercial insurance, staying updated isn't just a good practice—it's a professional necessity. There's an ongoing stream of market trends, policy changes, new products, and revised best practices. Being at the forefront of this information tidal wave provides you with the knowledge you need to offer your clients the best possible solutions. Remember, what you're really selling is not just a policy, but your expertise and guidance. And your expertise is worth only as much as your willingness to continuously update it.

One proven way to stay current is by earning reputable designations. Organizations like The National Alliance for Insurance Education & Research offer designations such as CIC (Certified Insurance Counselor) and CRM (Certified Risk Manager) that can elevate your expertise and credibility. The Institutes offer designations like CPCU (Chartered Property Casualty Underwriter) that delve deep into the nuances of property and casualty insurance, among other areas. The Risk and Insurance Management Society (RIMS) offers the RIMS-CRMP (Certified Risk Management Professional), which provides a competitive edge in risk management. These designations don't just add initials after your name; they offer rigorous curricula that keep you updated on the latest industry trends, and many require ongoing education to maintain.

Reading leading industry publications is another way to stay ahead. Whether it's *Risk & Insurance*, *Insurance Journal*, or other specialized magazines and blogs, subscribing to these outlets will keep you stay informed about the latest products, best practices, and emerging risks. Often, these publications are the first to report on legislative changes that could affect your clients, allowing you to proactively advise them on how to adjust their coverage.

Networking remains an invaluable source of current information. Associations like the Independent Insurance Agents & Brokers of America (Big "I") and the National Association of Professional Insurance Agents (PIA) offer state and national platforms for networking. These organizations often have their fingers on the pulse of local, state, and national policy changes. They also provide forums, events, and webinars where professionals can share insights, strategies, and predictions for the future. Being a part of these networks enables you to keep your ear to the ground, hear firsthand accounts of how trends are playing out in different markets, and share your own experiences and learn from others.

Don't underestimate the power of social networking forums either. LinkedIn groups and industry-specific online communities are excellent platforms where real-time discussions occur, allowing you to tap into collective wisdom. These discussions can often provide insider perspectives on market trends and emerging risks that you won't find in publications.

Clients, too, can be valuable sources of information. Their questions and concerns often raise issues that are worth investigating further. A client asking about cybersecurity coverage, for example, could prompt you to delve deeper into that area, helping you not just to answer that client's question but also to better advise future clients on that emerging risk.

The overarching message is that knowledge equates to value in the world of commercial insurance. The more you know, the better you can serve your clients and the more indispensable you become. So, make a firm commitment to continuous learning. Sign up for webinars, attend seminars, pursue designations, engage in networking, and devour reputable publications. Use these as tools to sharpen your expertise, anticipate client needs, and adapt to the dynamic insurance landscape. In doing so, you're not just bolstering your credentials; you're fortifying your role as an invaluable resource in a complex and fast-paced industry.

By mastering the art of relationship building, optimizing your time, and continuously enhancing your knowledge, you position yourself as an indispensable partner to your clients, paving the way for sustained success in the commercial insurance world. The following chapters will delve further into advanced techniques and strategies for the modern insurance producer.

Chapter 11: Ethical Selling: More Than Just Making a Deal

The Moral Compass in Commercial Sales

No matter how complex this industry seems, one pillar remains constant and that is ethics. While I have already addressed the importance of ethics earlier in this book, I feel compelled to underscore its significance once again. The moral compass in commercial sales isn't something that should merely guide your decisions; it should be the foundation upon which you build your entire practice. Ethical considerations should permeate every aspect of your work, from initial client conversations to policy recommendations and from claims handling to renewals. Prioritizing ethical behavior isn't just a noble endeavor; it's a practical one that solidifies trust, ensures legal and regulatory compliance, and fosters long-term success.

In a world inundated with endless choices, transparency can be your unique selling point. Transparency isn't just about disclosing the facts, it's also about being open regarding the implications of those facts. For example, explaining a policy's limitations or exclusions in layman's terms, so your clients understand what they're buying, is crucial. This way, you not only avoid any accusations of misrepresentation but also build a relationship grounded in trust and respect. Keep in mind that trust isn't a one-time deal; it is consistently reinforced or eroded with every client interaction. A single breach in ethics can cast a long shadow over your future dealings, not only with the affected client but often in the wider market, given the speed at which news, especially bad news, travels.

The ripple effect of ethical lapses can be much wider than you might anticipate. Suppose you indulge in even a single episode of mis-selling or fail to disclose pertinent information to a client. In that case, the consequences may not be limited to just client dissatisfaction or loss of business. Legal repercussions are often inevitable, and regulatory bodies take such lapses very seriously. Violations can result in fines, loss of license, and in extreme cases, criminal charges. Further, a damaged reputation in the industry may be irreparable or at least will take years to mend and could also impact your relationships with underwriters, carriers, and even your own colleagues.

Another dimension of ethics in commercial insurance involves how you deal with competitors. Competition is

The Ultimate Advantage

fierce, and the temptation to cut corners to get ahead is real. However, discrediting competitors unethically or engaging in deceptive practices such as quote manipulation can have severe consequences. These not only jeopardize your reputation but can also invite legal ramifications. Always remember, how you behave when you think nobody is watching is the true measure of your ethical stance.

The responsibility to operate ethically also extends to your role as an adviser to your clients. As their businesses grow, they look to you to identify new areas of risk and recommend appropriate coverage solutions. This involves not just up-to-date product knowledge but an in-depth understanding of their business requirements. It would be easy to recommend the most expensive coverage for the sake of a higher commission. Still, the ethical approach is to provide the coverage that most closely matches the client's needs, even if that does not result in the maximum possible revenue for you.

Ethical behavior is also about how you treat your colleagues and support staff within your organization. This includes being honest about your capabilities and respecting the contributions of others. Misleading your team about the potential value of a deal or minimizing the risks involved to win internal support does a Disservice to your colleagues, yourself, and ultimately, to your clients.

Being ethical also means staying committed to continuous learning. The more you know, the better you can serve your clients. Therefore, deliberately avoiding new information to maintain the status quo, or worse, to persist in outdated but profitable practices, is inherently unethical.

Finally, fostering an ethical culture isn't a one-person job; it's an organizational effort. While you can control your actions, encouraging a culture of ethics within your team and broader agency can amplify the impact. Agencies should offer regular training sessions on ethical considerations in the ever-changing insurance landscape, complete with real-world scenarios and potential grey areas. This type of education helps establish a universally understood ethical framework within which everyone operates, reducing the likelihood of lapses.

Ethics in commercial insurance sales is not just a topic for discussion in a training seminar or a chapter in a manual. It's the lens through which every decision should be viewed. Acting ethically not only benefits you in the long run but also serves your clients, supports your colleagues, and enriches the industry. Prioritizing ethical considerations is a win-win strategy that ensures that you don't just survive in this complex, competitive landscape, but thrive. It's not just about doing things right but about doing the right things— consistently and conscientiously.

Building a Reputation: Prioritizing Client Needs Over Short-Term Gains

In the fiercely competitive world of insurance, establishing a stellar reputation can be your greatest asset. And a cornerstone of that reputation is transparency, particularly in the handling of policy terms, costs, and potential limitations. Transparency is not merely a best practice; it's an ethos that must permeate every interaction with clients. The temptation to skirt over less favorable details for the sake of closing a deal is a short-sighted strategy that can have long-term repercussions. Misrepresenting or omitting facts is not only a breach of trust but can also lead to compliance issues, legal battles, and a tarnished reputation that can take years to rebuild.

The Ultimate Advantage

Transparency should extend beyond the initial policy discussions and into all facets of client interaction, from claims handling to policy renewals. Clients should feel comfortable asking any questions they may have and confident that they will receive straightforward, unbiased answers. When you're clear about the costs, potential limitations, and even the caveats of a policy, you earn your client's trust. It might seem counterintuitive, but disclosing less favorable details can actually work in your favor, validating your integrity and reliability as an advisor. While you may lose out on some short-term gains, the long-term benefits of being transparent far outweigh the immediate losses.

The notion of prioritizing long-term vision over short-term gains dovetails perfectly with this topic. Imagine you have two policy options for a client: one that earns you a higher commission in the short term but isn't necessarily the best fit for the client, and another that is ideal for the client but less profitable for you initially. While the temptation to opt for the former can be strong, especially in a sales-driven environment, the latter is the ethical and strategically wise choice. By selecting the option that best suits the client, you not only build trust but also lay the foundation for a long-term relationship. A client who feels you have their best interests at heart is likely to stick with you for years and may offer the opportunity for upsells, cross-sells, and referrals down the line, which can be more lucrative than any single transaction.

Finally, every action and recommendation you make should be rooted in a philosophy of client advocacy. Your role is not just to sell policies but to serve as a trusted advisor. This involves more than just recommending the best policies. It means understanding the client's business, staying updated on industry trends and changes that might affect them, and proactively offering solutions that align with their evolving needs. Whether it's suggesting ways to improve workplace safety, providing updates on regulatory changes, or offering new types of coverage that could benefit them, being an advocate solidifies your reputation as a trusted and valuable partner.

To sum this up, prioritizing transparency and long-term client relationships over short-term gains is not just an ethical choice but also a smart business strategy. It serves as a differentiation factor in a crowded marketplace, enabling you to build and maintain a reputation that can sustain and grow your business over time. This client-first approach ensures that your role evolves from a mere service provider to a valuable partner in your client's success. As the saying goes, "People do business with those they know, like, and trust." Prioritizing client needs and acting transparently ensures you check all three boxes, setting you up for long-term success in the competitive insurance industry. The question "Who do you want to be a hero to?" is a powerful concept developed by Dan Sullivan that serves as a guiding light in defining your role and relationships in business. It challenges you to focus on the groups or individuals to whom you want to bring extraordinary value. For a commercial insurance producer, this typically boils down to three main constituencies: the insurance carriers you represent, your agency, and most importantly, your clients.

Insurance Carriers: Being a "hero" to your insurance carriers requires a multi-faceted approach that goes beyond merely selling policies. You are essentially the intermediary between the carrier and the end customer, and thus, you play an integral role in shaping the carrier's market penetration, brand perception, and bottom line. Here's how to fulfill these roles effectively:

Understanding Products: A thorough understanding of your carrier's products is non-negotiable. It's not just about knowing what the products are, but also how they can be tailored to fit specific client needs. This ensures that you sell the right policies to the right clients, thereby reducing the risk of future claims and improving profitability for the carrier.

Articulating Value: You must be able to articulate why a particular policy from a particular carrier offers superior value compared to other products in the marketplace. This includes not only policy features but also the financial stability of the carrier, its customer service record, and any other factors that make it stand out. Essentially, you're a storyteller; the better the story, the easier the sale, and the happier the carrier is with your performance.

Market Penetration: Carriers often have target markets that they find especially valuable but challenging to penetrate. A hero producer will identify these opportunities and strategize on how best to introduce the carrier's offerings to these markets. Your local knowledge and industry connections can be invaluable here.

High-Quality Submissions: The submission process is where you can truly stand out. Accurate, complete, and well-documented submissions make the underwriter's job easier and increase the likelihood your client will get the best terms. An underwriter who trusts your submissions is more likely to give you beneficial terms, improving your close rate and profitability for the carrier.

Honesty and Integrity: Carriers place great value on producers who are honest about the limitations and strengths of both the clients they're representing and the products they're selling. Concealing information may yield short-term gains but can backfire spectacularly in the long term. An honest relationship builds trust, which is the cornerstone of a successful, long-term partnership.

Profitable Business: At the end of the day, carriers are in business to make a profit, and they rely on you to bring in business that achieves this goal. This doesn't just mean selling high-premium policies; it also means selling policies that are a good risk match for the carrier. An excellent producer understands the carrier's risk appetite and tailors client submissions accordingly.

High Close Rate: This signals your effectiveness as a salesperson, certainly, but it also signifies the appropriateness of the match between the client's needs and the carrier's offerings. A high close rate with minimal subsequent claims is a strong indicator of a producer who understands both sides of the equation well.

Regulatory Compliance: Given the highly regulated nature of the insurance industry, adhering to compliance requirements is critical. Whether it's about policy documentation, customer identification, or transaction recording, a lapse in compliance can lead to severe penalties for the carrier and can immediately break the trust you've built.

Feedback Mechanism: A producer in regular contact with clients is well-placed to provide feedback to carriers about how their products are perceived, what's working, and what could be improved. This can be invaluable business intelligence for a carrier.

By excelling in these areas, you directly align your success with that of your carriers. They will see you as not just a producer, but as a strategic partner. This is when you transition from being just another salesperson to being a hero in the eyes of your carriers. And heroes, as we know, are not only celebrated but also rewarded.

Your Agency:

Being a hero within your agency goes far beyond hitting your quarterly or annual sales targets. It's about embodying a holistic view of success that includes team building, mentorship, innovation, and above all, alignment with the agency's mission and values. Being a hero is not a solo effort but rather a symphony of strategic and harmonious actions that enhance the overall well-being of the organization. Let's delve deeper into what exactly an agency expects from a producer to earn this heroic status.

Sales Acumen and Business Development

While it's undeniable that sales targets are crucial, they are not the only measure of your value to the agency. In addition to consistently meeting or exceeding these targets, you should be focused on qualitative elements such as the types of accounts you're bringing in, their long-term value, and their fit with the agency's broader strategic goals. This also includes your ability to up-sell or cross-sell effectively, increasing the lifetime value of each client. Your aim should be to bring in business that aligns with the agency's growth strategy and provides a stable foundation for its financial health.

Leadership and Mentorship

As an experienced producer, one of your roles is to act as a mentor to junior staff. Whether formally or informally, sharing your industry knowledge, sales techniques, and strategies for overcoming challenges can be invaluable for new or less experienced team members. Your ability to mentor effectively not only adds value to the individuals you're coaching but also helps to lift the overall skill level within the agency, thereby increasing its competitive advantage.

Positive Work Culture and Ethical Conduct

Your behavior sets the tone for the culture within the agency. Practicing ethical conduct in all dealings, being respectful, open, and encouraging to colleagues, and contributing to a positive work environment are crucial. Your ethical stance not only improves the agency's reputation but also helps in attracting and retaining top talent. In an industry where reputation is everything, your exemplary conduct can be one of your most significant contributions to the agency.

Strategic Alignment

Being a hero means understanding the "big picture" of what the agency is trying to achieve and aligning your actions accordingly. This could involve identifying new market opportunities, recommending changes to internal processes to boost efficiency, or taking the initiative to launch a new service offering that fills a gap in the market. Strategic alignment is about ensuring that your day-to-day actions and longer-term plans both serve the agency's mission and vision.

Reliability and Consistency

Being a hero is often about the less glamorous aspects of the job: being reliable and consistent. When colleagues know they can depend on you to deliver what you promise, whether it's a small task or a major project, you become a stabilizing force within the agency. Your consistent performance gives management the confidence to make plans and projections based on the expectation of your continued success.

Innovation and Adaptability

The insurance industry is ever-changing. New market trends, technologies, and regulations constantly emerge, requiring quick adaptation. Your ability to adapt, innovate, and evolve makes you invaluable to your agency. Whether it's by adopting new technologies that streamline operations or by learning about emerging markets and trends that offer fresh opportunities, an innovative approach can significantly impact the agency's competitiveness and long-term success.

Being a hero in your agency is a multifaceted role that requires a combination of hard skills like sales acumen and soft skills like leadership, cultural contribution, and strategic alignment. As a producer, you're not just a cog in the machine; you're a linchpin that can significantly influence the success and the future direction of the agency. By excelling in these areas, you don't just build your success; you contribute to the collective success, earning you hero status within your agency.

Clients: Becoming a hero to your clients is perhaps the most significant role you can fulfill as a commercial insurance producer. Achieving this hero status requires a multi-dimensional approach that elevates the client relationship from a mere transactional interaction to a deeply rooted partnership. A true "hero" in the eyes of the client is not just a salesperson but a consultant, an advisor, and, most importantly, a trustworthy advocate. Let's dissect the key elements that make up this heroic approach.

Deep Understanding of Client Needs and the Industry

Being a hero starts with an in-depth understanding of your clients' needs. You should invest time and effort into learning about their industry, the challenges they face, and the specific risks that are unique to their type of business. This deep understanding will allow you to match them with insurance products that are not just good, but perfect for their situation. You'll need to keep up to date with changes in their industry that might affect their risk profile—such as regulatory changes, emerging risks like cybersecurity, or changes in the supply chain—and proactively recommend adjustments to their coverage as needed.

Transparency and Honesty

Your clients need to trust you implicitly, and nothing builds trust faster than honesty and transparency. This means you should be upfront about policy terms, limitations, and costs. If a client wants a policy that you know is not the best fit for their needs, your duty is to steer them towards the product that serves them best—even if it means less commission for you in the short term. In the long term, your honesty will be rewarded with client loyalty and referrals.

Exceptional Customer Service and Availability

Clients expect exceptional service before, during, and after the policy purchase. Your job doesn't end when the contract is signed; it's just the beginning. You should be available to answer questions, clarify concerns, and provide advice when needed. Rapid response times and effective solutions to their issues can set you apart from competitors. Moreover, you should offer regular check-ins or reviews to make sure that the policies are still serving their intended purpose and that the client is happy with your services.

Proactive Problem-Solving and Value-Addition

As an insurance hero, your mindset should be geared towards solving problems before they arise. This may involve educating your client about the emerging risks in their industry, suggesting preventive measures, or helping them develop a comprehensive risk management strategy. You could offer webinars, write-ups, or regular newsletters that provide valuable insights. The key is to offer ongoing value that extends well beyond the product you are selling.

Long-term Relationship Building

The Ultimate Advantage

Being a hero to your clients means thinking long term. The most fruitful client relationships in insurance are rarely transactional; it evolves from a sales person to a valued consultant. The aim is to build a partnership rooted in mutual respect and trust, where the client comes to see you as an indispensable part of their risk management team Over time, as their business grows and evolves, you will be there to guide them, adjust their coverage, and offer solutions that they hadn't even considered

No Immediate Financial Gain? No Problem

There will be times when what is in the best interest of your client may not offer any immediate financial gain for you. In such instances, the heroic thing to do is to act in the best interest of your client anyway. This could mean advising them to keep a policy that is less profitable for you but offers them better coverage for their needs. When clients see that you're willing to put their needs first, regardless of your immediate gain, you not only build trust but also fortify a long-term relationship.

Being a hero to your clients is an ongoing commitment that involves much more than just selling them a policy. It's about service, trust, problem-solving, and above all, placing their needs above your immediate gains. By doing so, you don't just create a client; you create a long-term business advocate who will see you as their go-to insurance hero.

So, what do these three groups have in common? They all want a hero who adds value, who goes beyond the expected, who treats their needs and objectives as paramount. This means that you have to understand these needs deeply, and tailor your offerings and actions accordingly. Dan Sullivan's question encourages you to create a win-win-win scenario, where you are contributing positively to each group's success. By identifying what each of these constituencies needs to see you as a hero, you can strategically guide your actions and decisions to meet and exceed those expectations, solidifying your own success in the process.

Chapter 12: The Three-Year Training Plan for a Producer, with KPIs and Goals

This chapter presents a structured approach to building a substantial book of business, aiming for $500,000 in revenue in three years. This journey also includes the pursuit of a Certified Insurance Counselor (CIC) designation, enhancing your credibility and expertise in the field. The plan is meticulously divided into quarterly goals, focusing on revenue growth, educational advancement, and strategic client engagement.

The beauty of this plan lies in its adaptability. While the revenue targets, educational milestones, and timelines are laid out, they are not set in stone. They serve as a framework that can and should be adjusted to suit your unique style, market dynamics, and personal growth pace. This plan is ambitious yet achievable, demanding but rewarding. It's designed to push you out of your comfort zone and into a space where significant professional growth is possible. After engaging with this plan, you should be well-equipped to outline a personalized strategy, keeping in mind that continuous refinement based on real-world experiences is key to success in this dynamic field.

Year 1: Foundation and Niche Identification

Q1 Goals:

Revenue Goal: Secure a minimum revenue of $2,000 per client and an average revenue per client of $2,500.
Education Goal: Start the first module of the CIC designation, focusing on personal lines.

- **Actions:**
- Identify two to three niches for specialization.
- Create a list of 100 prospects in the chosen niches.
- Average two meetings per week
- Make forty cold calls per week.
- Identify two Centers of Influence (COIs)

Q2 Goals:

Revenue Goal: $25,000 total; raise average revenue per client to $3,000.
Education Goal: Complete the first module and enroll in the second module focusing on commercial casualty.

- **Actions:**
- Refine prospect list to top 150.
- Average three meetings per week
- Make fifty cold calls per week.
- Identify two more COIs.

Q3 Goals:

Revenue Goal: $50,000 total; maintain average revenue per client of $3,000.
Education Goal: Complete the second module of CIC.

- **Actions:**
- Expand the list to 200 prospects.
- Average four meetings per week
- Make sixty cold calls per week.
- Build relationships with existing COIs.

Q4 Goals:

Revenue Goal: $80,000 total; aim for average revenue per client of $3,500.
Education Goal: Enroll in the third module focusing on commercial property.

- **Actions:**
- Refine list to top 200 prospects.

The Ultimate Advantage

- Average five meetings per week
- Make seventy cold calls per week.
- Solidify two new COI relationships.

Year 2: Expansion and Specialization

Q1 Goals:

Revenue Goal: $120,000 total; aim for average revenue per client of $4,000.
Education Goal: Complete the third CIC module.

- **Actions:**
- Keep the list updated with at least 200 prospects.
- Average six meetings per week
- Make eighty cold calls per week.
- Identify two new COIs.

Q2 Goals:

Revenue Goal: $170,000 total; maintain average revenue per client of $4,000.
Education Goal: Enroll in the fourth CIC module focusing on agency management.

- **Actions:**
- Average seven meetings per week
- Make ninety cold calls per week.
- Strengthen relationships with existing COIs.

Q3 Goals:

Revenue Goal: $230,000 total; maintain average revenue per client of $4,000.
Education Goal: Complete the fourth CIC module.

- **Actions:**
- Average eight meetings per week
- Make 100 cold calls per week.
- Secure partnerships through COIs

Q4 Goals:

Revenue Goal: $300,000 total; aim for average revenue per client of $4,500.
Education Goal: Enroll in the fifth CIC module focusing on life and health.

- **Actions:**
- Average nine meetings per week
- Establish long-term collaborations with COIs.

Year 3: Mastery and Scaling

Q1 Goals:

Revenue Goal: $360,000 total; aim for average revenue per client of $4,500.
Education Goal: Complete the fifth CIC module.

- **Actions:**
- Average ten meetings per week

The Ultimate Advantage

- Keep cold calls at 100 per week going forward.
- Leverage COIs for high value deals.

Q2 Goals:

Revenue Goal: $420,000 total; maintain average revenue per client of $4,500.
Education Goal: Review all modules.

- **Actions:**

- Average eleven meetings per week.
- Strengthen high value relationships.

Q3 Goals:

Revenue Goal: $460,000 total; aim for average revenue per client of $4,800.

- **Actions:**
- Average twelve meetings per week
- Leverage COIs for large contracts.

Q4 Goals:

Revenue Goal: $500,000 total; hit the ultimate goal of average revenue per client of $5,000.
Education Goal: Successfully obtain CIC designation.

- **Actions:**
- Average thirteen to fifteen meetings per week
- Fully leverage COIs for large, long-term contracts

Achieving a significant benchmark in commercial insurance sales necessitates a well-structured strategy and a commitment to diligently following that blueprint. This plan is perfect for a commercial insurance agent aiming for a $500,000 business portfolio by the third year.

Right Types of Clients: Understand the needs of your target demographic. Opt for businesses or industries where your expertise aligns, ensuring that they see the value in what you're offering. Make sure you are targeting accounts that generate the revenue you are looking for.

SMART Goal Setting: Develop Specific, Measurable, Achievable, Relevant, and Time-bound objectives. A clear plan with milestones can help you track progress and stay on course.

Action Plan: Detail the steps necessary to achieve your goals, including the resources required and a timeline. Regularly update and refine this plan based on your experiences and the feedback you receive.

Maximize Efforts: Dedicate time to continuous learning, improving your sales techniques, and understanding emerging industry trends.

Innovative Practices: Implement ideas that could make your service stand out and streamline your operations, ensuring a higher sales velocity.

In the pursuit of this training plan and revenue goals, there are certain key numbers and activities that you should consistently focus on. Maintaining a prospect list of at least 200 is crucial; this ensures that you have a sufficient pipeline to not just meet, but potentially exceed, your targets. A robust prospect list is your foundation for sustained growth and opportunity. Committing to making 100 cold calls a week is essential to keep this list dynamic and rich with potential. This level of activity is what keeps the 'hot prospects' at a healthy 200, ensuring a continuous stream of opportunities. Moreover, aiming for an average commission revenue of $5,000 per client simplifies your target to acquiring just 100 customers over three years. This breaks down to adding approximately 2.7 new clients per month—a challenging yet feasible goal. Remember, it's the consistent activity and engagement that leads to tangible results. While the idea of generating $500,000 in revenue in three years may seem daunting, it's important to recognize that with hard work and dedication, it is an attainable goal. The journey will be demanding, no doubt, but with a steadfast commitment to these key activities and numbers, you are setting the stage for remarkable success in the commercial insurance field.

Chapter 13: Building a Thriving Career as a Commercial Producer

Your journey as a commercial producer is akin to running a marathon, not a sprint. Each sale, each relationship, and every decision you make is a chisel strike, sculpting your legacy in the industry. The path may be long and arduous, but with perseverance, a clear vision, and strategic planning, the rewards can be monumental. It's not just about securing a significant deal or landing a big client, though those are certainly milestones to be celebrated. The real key to sustained success lies in the consistent growth and nurturing of a diverse client base, and in the cultivation of strong, lasting relationships.

The Long Game: Growing Your Portfolio and Client Base

The long game is all about strategic growth. It involves developing a diverse portfolio of clients, maintaining a steady flow of new prospects, and deepening relationships with existing clients.

Consistency Is Key

While landing significant deals and big clients can provide a boost to your revenue and reputation, it's the everyday activities that lay the foundation for long-term success. It's about consistently prospecting, meeting with clients, solving their problems, and adding value to their businesses. For example, rather than just closing a deal and moving on to the next one, take the time to follow up with your clients, understand their evolving needs, and provide solutions that help them succeed. By consistently demonstrating your commitment to their success, you reinforce your value as a trusted advisor, and lay the foundation for a long and fruitful partnership.

Referrals: A Powerful Tool for Growth

A satisfied client is your best advocate. When your clients are happy with your service, they are more likely to refer their network to you. These referrals can be a goldmine of new business opportunities. However, it's essential to be proactive in encouraging referrals. Don't just wait for them to happen organically. Make it a habit to ask satisfied clients for referrals and make it easy for them to refer potential clients to you by providing them with the necessary information and materials. Moreover, show your appreciation to clients who consistently provide referrals by recognizing them in some way, whether it's with a thank-you note, a small gift, or a referral fee.

Fostering Long-Term Relationships

The relationships you build with your clients are the cornerstone of your success as a commercial producer. It's not just about selling a policy; it's about becoming a trusted advisor to your clients. This involves understanding their business, their industry, and their unique risks and challenges. It means providing them with the right solutions at the right time and being there for them when they need you most.

Understanding Your Clients' Needs

To truly understand your clients' needs, you must immerse yourself in their world. Stay updated on the latest trends and developments in their industry. Regularly meet with your clients to discuss their current challenges, future plans, and how you can support them. For example, if you have a client in the construction industry, and there has been a recent increase in construction accidents in their area, meet with them and discuss the steps they can take to mitigate these risks, and provide them with the necessary insurance coverages.

Providing Value Beyond the Sale

Your relationship with your clients shouldn't end once the sale is made. Continually look for ways to add value to their business. This could be in the form of providing them with relevant industry insights, connecting them with potential business partners, or helping them manage their risks more effectively. For instance, if you notice that one of your clients has a gap in their risk management strategy, proactively offer them a solution, even if it doesn't result in an immediate sale. Your clients will appreciate your proactive approach, and it will reinforce your position as a trusted advisor.

Being Responsive and Available

In today's fast-paced world, being responsive and available to your clients is more important than ever. Make it a point to respond to your clients' inquiries and concerns promptly. If a client contacts you with a question or a problem, make it a priority to address it as soon as possible. If you don't have the answer right away, let them know that you are working on it and will get back to them as soon as possible. Your responsiveness shows your clients that you value their business and are committed to their success.

Your journey as a commercial producer is a marathon, not a sprint. It's about playing the long game, consistently growing and nurturing your client base, and fostering strong, lasting relationships. By understanding your clients' needs, providing value beyond the sale, and being responsive and available, you position yourself as a trusted advisor and set the stage for long-term success. Remember, each sale, each relationship, and every decision you make plays a role in sculpting your legacy in the industry. Stay consistent, stay proactive, and always look beyond the horizon.

Leveraging Testimonials, Case Studies, and Success Stories for Business Growth

Leveraging testimonials, case studies, and success stories can provide a critical edge in a competitive commercial insurance landscape. These powerful tools offer more than mere social proof; they are testimonies of your expertise, the effectiveness of your solutions, and your ability to deliver. Their influence on potential clients is often significant, helping to assuage concerns, build trust, and streamline the decision-making process. Here's a deep dive into how these tools can significantly contribute to your business growth:

Showcase Success: The Art and Impact of Client Success Stories

One of the most compelling ways to convince potential clients of your expertise and effectiveness is to share success stories from your existing clients. These narratives should focus on specific problems faced by the client, the solutions you provided, and the resulting outcomes. Did you help a manufacturing company reduce workplace accidents by recommending tailored policies? Maybe you assisted a retailer in navigating the complex legal landscape through comprehensive liability coverage? These stories, when shared with explicit permission from the clients involved, can be incredibly impactful.

Success stories have a human element, making them relatable and memorable. They can be shared through various channels: your website, email marketing campaigns, social media, or even in printed brochures. Furthermore, video interviews with satisfied clients discussing how you helped them can make the stories more immediate and emotionally engaging.

Encourage Testimonials

While success stories showcase the specific challenges and triumphs of individual clients, testimonials offer brief yet potent endorsements of your services. These usually come in the form of quotes that are easy to consume and share. Importantly, the source of the testimonial lends weight to the statement. A positive word from a well-known industry player can be a substantial asset.

The Ultimate Advantage

To maximize the impact, display these testimonials prominently on your marketing materials and website. They can be integrated into your homepage, included in client proposals, or even showcased in your office. Don't forget to diversify the types of testimonials you collect. While some may focus on your expertise, others might emphasize your excellent customer service or your knack for solving complex problems. The broader the range of praise, the more potential clients it will resonate with.

Documented Excellence: The Power of Case Studies

For complex issues that can't be fully captured by a testimonial or a brief success story, consider developing detailed case studies. These usually take the form of structured documents that lay out the client's challenge, your solution, and the results in a detailed, analytical format.

Case studies are particularly useful when your intervention led to quantifiable results—be it cost savings, increased revenue, or risk mitigation. By focusing on metrics and tangible outcomes, case studies not only demonstrate your depth of knowledge but also your aptitude for delivering measurable results.

For instance, you might develop a case study detailing how you helped a healthcare provider navigate the pitfalls of malpractice liability, thereby saving them from potential bankruptcy. In such a study, the quantifiable metrics could be the percentage decrease in legal costs or the number of malpractice claims.

In summary, these tools—success stories, testimonials, and case studies—serve as robust mechanisms for validating your services. They enable you to build trust and credibility in the market, attributes that are often intangible but immensely valuable. Therefore, adopting a structured approach to collect, showcase, and leverage these could significantly bolster your reputation and, by extension, your growth prospects. Leveraging these effectively can set you apart in a crowded marketplace, signaling to potential clients that you don't just promise—you deliver.

The journey of a commercial insurance producer is not for the faint of heart. It's a path filled with complex challenges and high-stakes decisions, one that demands an ever-evolving skill set and a steadfast commitment to ethical conduct. But for those who are up to the challenge, the rewards are equally substantial, offering not just financial benefits but also a deep sense of professional and personal fulfillment.

Firstly, let's talk about the financial rewards. The commercial insurance industry is an arena where financial compensation often mirrors your level of dedication and skill. Unlike many professions where the income potential may be capped, or the correlation between effort and reward is fuzzy, commercial insurance offers a transparent meritocracy. Those who work harder, constantly refine their skills, and focus on providing value to their clients don't only see a direct financial payoff but can even build a sustainable book of business that pays dividends over a long career. With each successful policy placement, with every problem solved for a client, and with the continued growth of your portfolio, you're not just earning a paycheck; you're building an asset—a reputation that can't easily be quantified.

However, the rewards are not merely financial. The role of a commercial producer offers an array of experiences that enrich you as a professional and as an individual. The landscape is so diverse—ranging from understanding specific industry risks to mastering the nuances of various insurance products—that learning never stops. The continuous pursuit of knowledge can be intellectually fulfilling, and there's a thrill in knowing that your expertise directly impacts the well-being and success of businesses. And let's not forget the obtainment of industry-specific designations like the CIC (Certified Insurance Counselor), which not only enhances your professional standing but also imbues a sense of personal achievement.

Additionally, commercial insurance is a relationship business. It's about people, about understanding their needs, solving their problems, and often becoming a trusted advisor beyond the confines of insurance. You become an integral part of the lives of your clients, understanding their businesses, predicting their risks, and providing solutions. This fosters a unique level of trust and respect that can be deeply gratifying. In a world where so many transactions are impersonal, the value of genuine relationships cannot be overstated.

The sense of personal satisfaction also extends to ethical practices. When you prioritize your client's needs, deliver on your promises, and conduct business in a transparent and ethical manner, you sleep better at night. There's an intrinsic reward in knowing you're doing right by your clients and, in turn, earning their unwavering trust. Ethical conduct in the commercial insurance space is not just about compliance; it's a cornerstone of long-term success.

Then there's the impact you make. Your work as a commercial producer goes beyond just the immediate transaction. You play a role in enabling businesses to operate confidently, grow, and even survive in challenging times. Each policy you place can mean a small business stays open, jobs are saved, and families are protected. The

The Ultimate Advantage

ripple effects of your work can often extend far beyond what's immediately visible.

In sum, the role of a commercial insurance producer is replete with challenges that test your intellectual, emotional, and ethical mettle. But these challenges are also what make the job so rewarding. Each day presents a new puzzle to solve, a new opportunity to make a meaningful impact. And in solving these puzzles, in seizing these opportunities, you're not just building a career—you're crafting a legacy. So, as you navigate through the hurdles and celebrate the victories, never lose sight of the core values and principles that make you who you are. They are your true north in a journey that is as fulfilling as it is demanding.

Chapter 14: Navigating Industry Events as a Commercial Insurance Agent

In today's fast-paced business environment, commercial insurance agents are constantly seeking avenues to differentiate themselves, strengthen their brand, and ultimately drive growth. Among the myriad opportunities available, industry events stand out as one of the most potent tools in an agent's arsenal. Specifically designed for sectors you are targeting, these events offer unparalleled advantages, but only if approached with the right mindset and preparation.

The Inherent Value of Industry Events

At a surface level, industry events might appear as mere gatherings where professionals network and exchange insights. However, for the discerning commercial insurance agent, they represent much more:

A Hub of Knowledge: With expert-led sessions, panels, and workshops, these events become a melting pot of the latest trends, innovations, and best practices in the industry. Attending such events ensures agents remain updated and can adapt to the ever-evolving demands of their clients.

Networking Goldmines: Beyond the obvious exchange of business cards, these events provide a platform for forming and nurturing long-term professional relationships. It's where collaborations are born, partnerships are forged, and valuable client relationships are initiated.

Showcasing Expertise: Especially in the sectors we are targeting, it's crucial for agents to establish themselves as thought leaders and experts in their field. Participating in, or even better, speaking at these events can amplify an agent's reputation and brand presence.

The Pitfall of Passive Participation

The Ultimate Advantage

It's essential to understand that while the potential benefits of industry events are vast, they aren't automatic. A passive approach—simply registering, attending a few sessions, and then leaving—yields minimal benefits. The mantra for success is active participation. This means not just being physically present but engaging, discussing, questioning, and even challenging when required.

Laying the Groundwork for Success

The difference between an average experience at an industry event and a transformative one lies in preparation. Here's a closer look at what this entails:

Research Is Key: Before attending the event, agents should familiarize themselves with the event's agenda, the speakers, the companies that will be represented, and even the attendees if possible. This knowledge allows for tailored interactions and can guide an agent on which sessions to prioritize.

Setting Clear Objectives: Before setting foot at the event, it's crucial to have clear goals. Whether it's meeting potential clients, understanding new industry regulations, or scouting for partnership opportunities, having defined objectives ensures time at the event is spent productively.

Pre-Event Outreach: If there's access to an attendee list or you anticipate that certain key individuals or firms will attend, reaching out in advance can set the stage for more meaningful in-person interactions. A simple email introducing yourself and expressing eagerness to discuss mutual interests can break the ice and pave the way for fruitful discussions during the event.

Practical Logistics: This might sound basic, but ensuring one has all the necessary materials—be it business cards, brochures, or even a well-rehearsed elevator pitch—can make a world of difference.

The Role of Strategic Execution

Once groundwork has been laid, the next step is executing the plan. This means navigating the event with a mix of flexibility and adherence to one's goals. It's about finding the right balance between attending sessions, networking, taking breaks to reflect, and ensuring one remains proactive throughout.

Here's a comprehensive guide for commercial insurance agents on how to effectively navigate industry events.

Securing a Speaking Slot

To truly make an impact at an industry event, consider aiming for a speaking slot. Not only does it position you as an authority figure, but it also guarantees visibility among attendees.

In the bustling sphere of industry events, securing a speaking slot can be a game-changer for professionals wanting to establish authority and share knowledge. For those in the commercial insurance sector, particularly agents, two topics stand out as immensely valuable for attendees: the art of selecting insurance through an agent-centric approach and the behind-the-scenes mechanics of commercial insurance.

Choosing the Agent First: A Paradigm Shift in Insurance Selection

Traditionally, many business owners have approached insurance as a commodity, hunting for the best-priced bid. However, this can be a misguided approach. Here's why prioritizing the agent over the premium is a smarter strategy:

Understanding TCOR (Total Cost of Risk): While shopping for the more affordable premium might seem like a straightforward way to save costs, it's only a part of the bigger picture. By focusing on TCOR, which encompasses various factors including premiums, risk management costs, and indirect costs of claims, business owners can achieve a more comprehensive understanding of their expenses. An experienced agent will guide businesses in analyzing their TCOR and strategizing accordingly.

Building a Trusting Relationship: Insurance isn't a one-off purchase. It's a crucial partnership that should evolve as a business grows. By choosing an agent first, businesses can ensure continuity, receiving advice tailored to their changing needs over the years.

Customized Approach: Every business has its unique set of risks. An agent who understands a company's industry, challenges, and vision will be better equipped to provide bespoke solutions.

Secrets to Commercial Insurance: Demystifying the Process

Diving into the intricacies of commercial insurance can be a revelation for many business owners. By understanding the mechanics of how rates are set, the role of reinsurance, and the dynamics between agents and carriers, businesses can make informed decisions.

Setting the Rates: Insurance rates aren't plucked out of thin air. They're determined based on a combination of factors, including industry data, claims history, and risk assessments. Knowledge about these can empower businesses in negotiations and in understanding their premium breakdowns.

The Role of Reinsurance: Reinsurance might sound like industry jargon, but it's a critical component. It's essentially insurance for insurance companies, providing them with protection against significant losses. By understanding how reinsurance impacts premiums and the overall stability of their insurer, businesses can better appreciate its importance.

The Dual Sales Challenge: Contrary to popular belief, agents don't just "sell" to clients. They also need to convince carriers that a particular business is a worthy risk. This dual selling process is a dance of negotiation, and businesses benefit when they have a seasoned agent who can adeptly manage both sides.

The One-Quote Dilemma: Many business owners aren't aware that insurance carriers typically provide a quote to just one agent, blocking others. This underscores the importance of choosing an agent early in the process. An early selection ensures that the agent, who understands a business's nuances, gets the all-important first quote.

Securing That Coveted Speaking Slot

Breaking into the world of speaking at events can be challenging, even for seasoned professionals. It's not just about expertise and experience; it's about strategy, perseverance, and tact. Whether you're aiming to be the speaker at a keynote address or a breakout session, there are methods to increase your chances of getting noticed and selected by event organizers.

Persistence Is Key

First and foremost, understand that being persistent doesn't equate to being pushy. It's about being continually present in the organizers' purview. If you've sent a pitch and haven't heard back in a few weeks, follow up. It's easy for emails to get lost in the shuffle, especially if the event is sizable. By reminding organizers of your interest and expertise, you're keeping your proposal active in their minds.

Build a Genuine Relationship with Organizers

If your goals include speaking at industry events in the future, make preparations now to make connections with the organizers and leadership for the events. Whenever you attend events, make a point of networking with the organizers at industry gatherings. When you're already on friendly terms, pitching becomes more of a conversation than a cold call. Instead of approaching event organizers with a one-sided mindset, work on cultivating a genuine relationship. Volunteer your time or serve on a committee, so that you become known and develop your reputation as being highly-skilled in your field and personable. Consider what you can do to be helpful to the organizers too.

Offer to Assist at the Event

Organizing an event is an intricate task, with countless moving parts. By offering your assistance, even in capacities other than speaking, you're positioning yourself as an asset. This could mean moderating a panel, helping with registrations, or even assisting in logistical tasks. When you're present and helpful, organizers will likely remember your enthusiasm and commitment when considering speakers for future events.

Be Ready as a Backup

The reality of event organizing is that things don't always go as planned. Speakers can cancel at the last minute due to unforeseen circumstances. Herein lies an opportunity: position yourself as a reliable backup. Even if organizers tell you their slots are filled, express your willingness to be on standby.

The Ultimate Advantage

Imagine the relief an organizer would feel, amidst the panic of a last-minute cancellation, knowing they have a prepared, knowledgeable speaker ready to step in. It showcases not just your expertise, but also your adaptability and commitment. This gesture can also provide a foot in the door, and even if you don't end up speaking at that particular event, the organizers will likely remember your flexibility and consider you for future opportunities.

Showcase Your Expertise

While persistence and adaptability are essential, nothing beats genuine expertise. Regularly update your professional profiles, like LinkedIn, with recent talks or workshops you've conducted. Publish articles or blog posts on the topics you're passionate about. By establishing yourself as a thought leader in your domain, you make your pitch more appealing to organizers.

Tailor Your Pitch

Generic pitches are easily spotted and quickly dismissed. Instead of sending a one-size-fits-all proposal, tailor your pitch to each event. Understand the event's theme, the audience's demographics, and the kind of sessions they've had in the past. Align your topic accordingly, demonstrating that you've done your homework and are genuinely invested in adding value to their event.

Gather Testimonials

If you've spoken at events before, gather testimonials. Feedback from previous attendees or organizers can significantly bolster your pitch. It provides an external validation of your speaking abilities and the value you bring to an event.

Use Video to Your Advantage

The Ultimate Advantage

In a world where content is consumed visually, having a video reel of your previous talks can be a game-changer. It allows organizers to get a sense of your presentation style, your command of the subject, and how you engage with an audience. It doesn't have to be a professionally edited reel; even snippets from seminars or workshops can serve the purpose.

Securing a speaking slot at an industry event is as much about strategy as it is about expertise. By building genuine relationships, showcasing your adaptability, and consistently demonstrating your expertise, you not only increase your chances of being selected but also lay the foundation for long-term partnerships with event organizers. Remember, each "no" is a step closer to a "yes," and with persistence and tact, you can navigate the competitive landscape of speaking opportunities.

Industry events can be transformative platforms, especially when speakers can shed light on lesser-known areas. By educating business owners on the nuanced world of commercial insurance, not only are you positioning yourself as a thought leader, but you're also building trust, paving the way for long-lasting partnerships.

Preparation Is Key

Industry events, with their potent mix of networking, knowledge sharing, and brand exposure, are invaluable for professionals across various domains. However, their true potential is harnessed not just by showing up but by laying down a robust strategy well in advance. The efficacy of your event attendance is predominantly determined by the groundwork you do long before you set foot at the venue.

The Power of the Attendee List

One of the first and most crucial steps to this preparatory phase is acquiring the attendee list. This document is not merely a list of names but a goldmine of opportunities. Here's why:

Identifying Potential Opportunities: With the attendee list in hand, you can discern potential clients, partners, or even competitors. A cursory glance might tell you the companies attending, but a deeper dive can provide insights into the decision-makers, influencers, or emerging players in your industry.

Enabling Preliminary Outreach: Armed with this information, you can begin your outreach even before the event starts. This could be in the form of personalized emails introducing yourself, expressing your interest in meeting them, or sharing resources that might be beneficial for their perusal. It's all about setting the stage for a more meaningful interaction during the event.

Leveraging the List for Tailored Strategies

Having the attendee list isn't just about knowing who's coming; it's about how you use that information to tailor your approach.

Pre-Scheduling Meetings: Instead of leaving meetings to chance encounters or packed event schedules, pre-schedule them. With the attendee list, you can determine who you absolutely must meet and then set up times in advance. This ensures that you get face time with key individuals and aren't left navigating through crowded event halls hoping to bump into them.

Promote Your Speaking Session: If you have a speaking slot or are conducting a workshop, the attendee list can help promote it. Send out invites to individuals or companies that would benefit most from your session. By giving them a heads-up, you're ensuring they block out that time to attend your talk.

Teasers and Sneak Peeks: Are you launching a product? Or perhaps you have an exciting offer at your booth? Use the attendee list to send out teasers or sneak peeks. It could be a short video, a promotional offer, or even a behind-the-scenes look at your preparations. The aim is to generate buzz and curiosity. So, when attendees are deciding which booths to visit or where to spend their time, your name is already on their list.

Customize Your Interactions: With knowledge of who's attending, you can also customize how you interact. Maybe a potential client has specific needs, and you can prepare a tailored pitch. Perhaps there's a partner you've been hoping to collaborate with, and you can create a proposal in advance. The attendee list helps you move from generic interactions to personalized conversations.

The importance of early preparation in maximizing the effectiveness of industry events cannot be stressed enough. With a proactive approach, especially leveraging tools like the attendee list, you ensure that your time at the event is productive, meaningful, and lays the groundwork for tangible results. Remember, in the world of events, success is determined as much by the strategy you craft beforehand as by your actions on the actual day.

Targeting the Right Audience

Walking into an industry event can often feel like venturing into a bustling marketplace. With possibly hundreds or even thousands of attendees, the sheer volume can be overwhelming. But, much like a marketplace, the value you derive isn't in the number of stalls you visit, but in the quality of interactions you have. How then, amidst the sea of attendees, do you ensure meaningful and impactful exchanges? The answer lies in a clearly defined strategy.

The Art of Segmentation: Crafting Your List

Before the event, it's essential to get your hands on an attendee list. This list is your roadmap, but much like a map, its utility lies in your ability to read it.

Categorizing Attendees: Not all attendees are created equal, and your interaction strategy needs to mirror this reality. Begin by segmenting your list into different categories. Who among them are potential leads? Who could be future partners? Who are the influencers or thought leaders in your industry? By identifying these categories, you're setting the stage for targeted interactions.

Prioritization: Once segmented, prioritize your interactions. Your time at the event is limited, and you want to ensure that you're spending the majority of it with high-value contacts. This isn't to say you ignore the rest, but by focusing on your top-tier contacts, you're maximizing the potential return on your time investment.

Active Engagement: Beyond Passive Networking

While having a clear list of who you want to interact with is essential, equally crucial is how you engage.

Participation in Sessions: Merely attending sessions isn't enough. Be an active participant. Whether it's a panel discussion, a workshop, or a keynote, ensure your presence is felt. Ask questions, offer insights, or even challenge viewpoints if you feel it's warranted. Active participation not only enhances your learning but also makes you more visible.

Engage in Discussions: Industry events are ripe with discussions, both formal and informal. Don't shy away from them. Engage in meaningful conversations, share your experiences, and listen to others. These interactions often lead to valuable insights, partnerships, and even business opportunities.

Making Yourself Accessible: While you should be proactive in seeking out interactions, also ensure you're accessible to others who might want to reach out. Wear your name badge prominently, make sure you're available during networking breaks, and even consider setting up a designated meet-up point or time for potential interactions.

Leveraging Technology: Many industry events now have dedicated apps or platforms for attendees. Use them to set up meetings, join discussions, or even share resources. Being tech-savvy at such events can significantly amplify your reach and effectiveness.

Industry events are a convergence of opportunities. But, like any opportunity, the value you derive is directly proportional to the effort you put in. By segmenting your attendee list and actively engaging, you're not just attending an event; you're crafting an experience. An experience that is rich in interactions, insights, and potential opportunities. Remember, in the vast ocean of attendees, it's not about meeting everyone but meeting the right ones. And with a clear strategy, you can ensure just that.

To Booth or Not to Booth

The Ultimate Advantage

At industry events, a booth serves as a tangible representation of a brand's presence. It's a dedicated spot to showcase what a brand offers, interact with attendees, and leave a lasting impression. But as with anything, setting up a booth has its advantages and challenges. Before diving into the world of booths, it's crucial to weigh its pros and cons to make the best decision based on your goals.

Advantages of Setting up a Booth

Visibility and Brand Recognition: One of the most significant advantages of having a booth is the visibility it provides. A well-placed, uniquely designed booth can draw attention, making attendees curious about what's on offer. It can be an excellent opportunity for brand exposure, ensuring attendees remember your company long after the event is over.

Dedicated Point of Contact: A booth serves as a fixed point of reference for attendees. Whether someone wants to ask detailed questions, offer feedback, or discuss potential partnerships, they know where to find you. It streamlines interactions and ensures that interested parties have an easy way to connect.

Promotional Opportunities: A booth is more than just a space; it's a promotional platform. It provides a chance to distribute materials like brochures and business cards. Moreover, giving away branded swag—be it pens, notebooks, or even USBs—can be a fantastic way to keep your brand in attendees' minds.

Engaging Activities: To enhance footfall, booths can incorporate various engagement techniques. Consider offering a keg of beer or other beverages, which can act as a magnet for attendees looking for a quick break. Booth games like raffles or ring tosses can also draw crowds. These activities not only increase engagement but also offer a more relaxed environment to start a conversation. Giveaways, particularly unique or valuable ones, can also generate buzz and entice attendees to visit.

Challenges of Booths and How to Overcome Them

Cost Consideration: Renting space, designing a booth, and procuring promotional materials can be costly. This expenditure becomes even more pronounced for smaller businesses or startups. However, this can be mitigated by sharing booth space with a complementary company or finding sponsors to cover some of the costs. It's also essential to view the booth as an investment, one that can lead to potential leads, partnerships, and sales.

Manpower Requirement: Manning a booth requires resources. It means that some team members will be anchored to the booth instead of attending sessions or networking freely. To counteract this, consider having a roster system. Schedule shifts so that everyone gets a chance to experience the event while ensuring the booth is always staffed.

Static Engagement: One of the inherent challenges of a booth is that it's stationary. You're dependent on attendees walking over and engaging. To overcome this, proactive measures can be adopted. Aside from the previously mentioned engaging activities, consider having a team member walk around the event, directing attendees to your booth, or promoting a scheduled activity at your booth, like a product demo or a quick workshop.

While booths can be a significant asset, their effectiveness is contingent upon how they are utilized. A booth should never be a passive element. Instead, it should be dynamic, actively pulling attendees in and offering them value. By understanding the challenges and leveraging the advantages, companies can ensure their booth isn't just a space but a highlight of the event.

Optimize External Events

In today's digital-centric business world, the significance of personal interactions remains timeless. Events like golf tournaments, charity dinners, and social gatherings present unique opportunities for professionals to foster relationships outside the confines of boardrooms and emails. While the potential at these events is vast, the key to successful networking lies in one's approach and genuine intent.

The Allure of External Events

Stepping away from the usual office setup, external events offer a refreshing environment for relationship-building. Golf tournaments, for example, may revolve around the sport, but the true essence lies in the shared moments, the camaraderie formed on the green, and the memories made. Dinners, with their relaxed ambiance, set the stage for profound conversations, allowing participants to delve deeper into topics and forge meaningful connections.

Charity galas, community get-togethers, and other social events serve as melting pots of diverse individuals and ideas. Here, shared passions and interests form the cornerstone of potential collaborations and business relationships.

Optimizing Your Engagement

While there's room for spontaneity, having a strategy can help maximize your networking opportunities. Consider the following:

Diversify Your Group: It's natural to gravitate towards familiar faces, but restricting yourself to your immediate circle can be limiting. Aim for diversity in your group.

The Ultimate Advantage

Include potential clients, existing customers, and professionals from varied backgrounds. This not only enriches the conversation but also paves the way for organic discussions about your offerings.

Seek Genuine Interactions: Authenticity is invaluable. Instead of starting a conversation with a transactional mindset, focus on building rapport. Listen actively, share personal stories, inquire genuinely, and be present in the conversation. When connections are forged on sincerity, they often transition into enduring professional partnerships.

Tailoring Your Approach to Different Events

Every event has its unique vibe and demands a specific approach:

Golf Tournaments: While the sport is central, it's the shared experience that counts. Use the game as a backdrop to understand your companions better, explore mutual interests, and let business discussions arise spontaneously.

Dinners: These gatherings, devoid of strict agendas, encourage open dialogues. Engage deeply, explore potential collaborations, and use the opportunity to gather insights or feedback.

Charity Galas & Social Gatherings: With a mix of personalities and purposes, these events are perfect for broadening one's horizons. Engage in varied discussions, contribute meaningfully, and always be open to learning from others.

In an era dominated by virtual meetings and digital correspondences, external events reaffirm the unmatched value of personal connections. Whether it's the camaraderie at a golf event, the intimate discussions during

The Ultimate Advantage

a dinner, or the vibrant energy of a charity gala, such events are treasure troves for genuine networking. Approach them with an open heart, prioritize real connections, and witness these relationships bloom both personally and professionally. After all, amidst a world of automated responses and templated pitches, authenticity remains the most compelling proposition.

Successfully navigating industry events as a commercial insurance agent requires more than just attending. With strategic preparation and genuine engagement, these events can become significant growth catalysts for agents looking to scale their operations. Whether it's through securing a coveted speaking slot, actively networking, or leveraging external events, the potential for making meaningful connections is immense. So, the next time you're heading to an industry event, remember plan, engage, and capitalize.

Chapter 15: Embracing Modern Technology: A Guide for the Commercial Insurance Agent

As commercial insurance agents venture into the contemporary digital realm, they encounter a diverse array of technological tools. These tools, from Customer Relationship Management (CRM) platforms to Artificial Intelligence (AI) assistance, are quintessential assets for agents striving to optimize their workflow and amplify their client services.

CRMs, which have seen significant advancements over the years, enable agents to maintain systematic records of clients, track their interactions, and even predict potential client behavior using predictive analytics. The role of AI in the insurance sector is expanding, offering automation of mundane tasks, providing 24/7 chatbot assistance, and aiding in risk assessments. Furthermore, AI's integration with other technologies is redefining the efficiency and scope of services that insurance agents can provide.

However, while discussing these technological marvels, it's pivotal to understand that the tech landscape is in perpetual flux. Technologies evolve, sometimes rendering earlier versions obsolete in short periods. Case in point, a glance at the last few decades reveals multiple technologies that have profoundly impacted industries and subsequently been phased out or radically transformed. For insurance agents, this means that while specific tools and platforms might undergo changes, the core philosophy behind leveraging technology remains constant: to enhance their capabilities, be more efficient, and offer superior client services.

Moreover, the "Law of Accelerating Returns" posits that technological change is exponential rather than linear, leading to rapid advancements. Thus, it's not just about adopting the latest tech but also about staying adaptable and continually upskilling.

So, as agents weave their strategies amidst this digital revolution, it's essential to stay rooted in the foundational principle: the use of technology should always augment human capabilities, not replace them. Whether it's the rise of AI or the next big tech wave post-AI, the central tenet remains to utilize these tools to create genuine value for clients.

One could liken this to a craftsman employing various instruments. The tools might vary or get increasingly sophisticated over time, but the artisan's goal is consistent— to craft impeccable pieces. Similarly, commercial insurance agents, while having their fingers on the pulse of evolving tech, must ensure they're harnessing it to foster genuine connections, offer insightful solutions, and build trust.

While agents must stay informed and agile in this ever-shifting technological paradigm, their focus should remain on how to best serve their clients, leveraging technology as a means to that end. Agents are, after all, not just tech-users but relationship-builders, solution-finders, and trust-creators in a complex ecosystem where human touch and technology must harmoniously coalesce. The beacon guiding this journey? A steadfast commitment to principles over fleeting trends.

Customer Relationship Management (CRM) Systems

In an age where digital tools are reshaping businesses, Customer Relationship Management (CRM) systems have emerged as game-changers. They've evolved from being mere data repositories to dynamic platforms that provide holistic solutions to insurance agents. To understand this transition, it's pivotal to dig deeper into what modern CRMs offer.

Today's CRMs are not just digital filing cabinets. They are highly sophisticated platforms that encapsulate the entirety of a client's journey with a business. From the initial inquiry to post-sale services, a CRM can map, track, and facilitate every touchpoint. Why has this shift occurred? As the business world became more interconnected and competitive, the emphasis shifted from mere transactional engagements to building and maintaining long-lasting relationships with clients.

One of the standout features of contemporary CRMs is their ability to facilitate personalized interactions. Gone are the days when interactions were generic and lacked a personal touch. With modern CRMs, agents can store intricate details about their clients, including past interactions, preferences, and specific policy details. This enables agents to tailor their communications precisely to the client's needs and preferences, ensuring every interaction feels personal and attentive. Personalization not only enhances client satisfaction but also fosters loyalty, an asset invaluable in today's competitive marketplace.

Apart from personalization, automated follow-ups are another pivotal feature of modern CRMs. In the hustle and bustle of daily operations, agents can overlook crucial touchpoints like policy renewals or periodic check-ins. However, with automation features in CRMs, agents can set reminders well in advance. These reminders ensure that no opportunity slips through the cracks, whether it's a chance to renew a policy, upsell a service, or simply check in on a client's satisfaction levels.

But why is all of this important? In essence, it's about trust. Clients want to feel valued and recognized. They crave interactions where businesses see them as individuals and not just another entry in a database. By using modern CRMs, agents can consistently offer this level of personalized service, demonstrating to clients that their needs and preferences are not just acknowledged but are at the forefront of every interaction.

As businesses grapple with the challenges of a digital-first world, the role of tools like CRMs cannot be overstated. They're not just facilitating business operations; they're revolutionizing how businesses perceive and interact with their most valuable asset—their clients. As the landscape of client interactions continues to evolve, it's clear that CRMs will remain pivotal, ushering businesses into a new era of personalized, attentive, and efficient service.

Data Sources for Benchmarking

In today's dynamic digital landscape, characterized by the relentless surge of information, adopting a data-driven approach is not just an advantage—it's a necessity. Information is power, and those who harness it efficiently can navigate the complexities of the modern business world with enhanced precision and foresight.

Consider the concept of Client Benchmarking. In the past, businesses made decisions based on intuition or limited available data. Today, professionals have an array of industry reports, analytics platforms, and real-time data collection tools at their disposal. Through these mediums, companies can gauge a client's risk profile in comparison to their market counterparts. Such insights allow businesses to tailor services, adjust strategies, and provide solutions that directly address the client's unique position in the marketplace. By leveraging comprehensive data sources, businesses can derive meaningful patterns and trends that were previously obscured or unrecognized.

Then there's Prospective Targeting. In a market that's continually evolving, staying a step ahead is pivotal for sustained success. Through adept data analysis, businesses can pinpoint industries or specific enterprises that are either underserved or burdened with exorbitant premiums. Once identified, these insights empower companies to strategically position their offerings. They can craft personalized pitches, develop bespoke solutions, or even restructure pricing models. In essence, a data-centric approach not only identifies gaps in the market but provides the tools and insights to bridge these gaps effectively.

The rise of such data-driven strategies is not just a phase—it's the reflection of an evolving business paradigm. Data has become the bedrock upon which businesses stand, driving decision-making processes, shaping organizational cultures, and fostering innovation. The age-old adage, "knowledge is power," has never been more pertinent. But today, it's not just about possessing knowledge; it's about efficiently harnessing, interpreting, and applying it.

However, it's crucial to note that while data offers a treasure trove of insights, it's only as valuable as the tools and minds deciphering it. Businesses must invest in robust analytics platforms, continually upskill their workforce, and foster a culture that's not just data-aware but data-inclined. As the digital age marches forward, the divide between those who adopt a data-driven ethos and those who don't will widen, with the former positioned for success and the latter at risk of obsolescence.

The age of information mandates a shift in perspective. It beckons businesses to move from intuition-based decision-making to an era where every decision, strategy, and move is rooted in concrete data. Such an approach not only offers precision but ensures adaptability in a world characterized by constant change.

Presentation Software

In the commercial insurance industry, captivating potential clients requires more than just a spoken pitch. Engaging visual presentations can elevate your proposal, making it memorable and convincing. Presentation software, especially popular platforms like PowerPoint, Prezi, and Canva, have proven invaluable in this respect.

Interactive Proposals: Modern clients appreciate interactivity. They want presentations that they can engage with, rather than passive slideshows. The traditional format of bullet points and static images, while informative, may not be enough to captivate your audience. Instead, consider:

Videos: Short, impactful videos can convey a message succinctly, breaking the monotony of a slide-based presentation. A video could highlight client testimonials or demonstrate the real-world impact of the coverage you're offering.

Infographics: A well-designed infographic can distill complex insurance data into an easily digestible visual. This can be particularly useful for illustrating coverage scenarios or statistical advantages.

Interactive Elements: Platforms like Prezi offer the option to incorporate interactive elements. This could be clickable areas that delve deeper into specific topics or even interactive Q&A segments that can be tailored on-the-fly based on audience responses.

Template Consistency: Branding is key in the insurance industry. Maintaining a consistent brand image throughout your presentations reinforces professionalism and makes your agency recognizable. A few ways to achieve this include:

Professional Templates: Platforms like Canva and Prezi offer a wide array of professional-looking templates designed for business presentations. These can be customized to align with your agency's colors, logo, and overall branding.

Branding Elements: Insert your agency's logo on every slide, utilize consistent fonts, and adhere to a color scheme that matches your brand identity.

Consistent Messaging: Beyond visual elements, ensure that the content of your presentations is aligned with your agency's mission, vision, and core values. This consistency in messaging reinforces trust and positions your agency as a dependable partner in commercial insurance.

The realm of commercial insurance is fiercely competitive. It's no longer sufficient to rely on word of mouth or written proposals alone. Embracing modern presentation tools can be the differentiating factor that sets your agency apart. Whether you're pitching to a small business or a large conglomerate, a compelling, interactive, and consistent presentation can be the key to securing their trust and business. The tools are at your fingertips; it's time to harness their power to elevate your proposals to new heights.

Email Campaigns

The evolution of digital marketing has provided businesses with a myriad of tools, and among the most powerful is email marketing. However, while reaching clients directly through their inbox has undeniable potential, it's crucial to ensure that your strategies are ethical and beneficial to the recipient.

Ethical Email Prospecting: Building trust is at the core of any successful business-client relationship, and ethical email practices lay that foundation:

Consent Is Paramount: Only send emails to individuals who've opted in. Unsolicited emails not only harm your brand's image but can also lead to legal complications.

Transparency: Clearly state the purpose of your email and provide a straightforward way for recipients to unsubscribe if they wish.

Accuracy: Ensure the information shared is accurate, unbiased, and not misleading. Avoid exaggerating benefits or making unsupported claims.

Ebooks as Value Addition: Offering free ebooks can be a win-win situation. It positions your business as a thought leader while providing clients with valuable insights:

- **Relevance Is Key:** Your ebook should address common concerns or challenges faced by your target audience. It can be a guide, a set of best practices, or an industry-specific analysis.

- **High Quality:** An ebook represents your brand. Ensure it's well-researched, professionally designed, and devoid of errors. Incorporating tips to make it lead-generating can be beneficial.

Segmentation: Delivering personalized content enhances engagement. Tools like Mailchimp and HubSpot can help segment your audience based on their interests, behaviors, or demographics:

Tailored Messages: Personalization has been shown to increase open rates. It ensures the recipient feels acknowledged and valued.

The Ultimate Advantage

Regular Updates: As your client base grows and evolves, regularly update your segmentation criteria to reflect their changing needs and preferences.

Engagement Analytics: To refine your email marketing approach, understanding your campaign's performance is crucial:

Open Rates: This metric helps determine if your subject line is compelling enough. A low open rate might indicate that the subject line isn't resonating or that emails are being directed to spam.

Click-Through Rates (CTR): A high CTR indicates your content is engaging, while a low rate might suggest that the email content isn't relevant or convincing enough.

Feedback Loop: Use these metrics to constantly improve. If a particular strategy results in high engagement, consider implementing similar techniques in future campaigns.

The power of email as a prospecting tool is undeniable. However, with great power comes responsibility. By ensuring that your strategies are rooted in ethical practices and by offering genuine value in the form of resources like ebooks, you're not just aiming for short-term gains. Instead, you're building long-lasting relationships based on trust and mutual benefit. Always remember, in the realm of digital marketing, genuine value and ethical considerations often translate to sustained success.

Social Media and Blog Posts

In the modern digital age, an expansive portion of your clientele is actively using social media platforms. This presents a tremendous opportunity to engage them effectively and establish authority in your domain. Let's explore methods and specific examples of how businesses, especially those dealing with risk management, can achieve these goals:

Sharing Insights on LinkedIn and Twitter:

Industry News: Post about a recent merger in the risk management sector, along with a brief analysis. Example: "The merger between Company A and Company B signals a shift in the risk management landscape. Here's what it could mean for small businesses. #RiskManagementNews"."

Regulatory Changes: Share updates about any modifications in industry regulations. For instance, "New regulatory changes in EU risk management standards will be effective in July. Here's a quick breakdown of what companies need to know. #RiskRegulationUpdate"

Risk Management Tips: Provide actionable advice, like, "Ensuring regular audits can minimize unforeseen risks. Here's a step-by-step guide on conducting efficient risk audits. #RiskManagementTips"."

In-Depth Blog Articles:

Risk Management Topics: Write an article elucidating the significance of holistic risk assessment, drawing on real-life examples. "A Comprehensive Look at How Company X's Holistic Risk Assessment Saved Them During the 2020 Financial Dip"."

Policy Nuances: Explore the intricacies of various risk management policies, offering a comparison for readers. "Comparing Policy A vs. Policy B: Which Offers Better Risk Coverage for Tech Startups?"."

Case Studies: Use real-life examples to showcase effective risk management practices. For instance, "A Deep Dive into How Company Y Navigated Regulatory Hurdles in 2022 Using Proactive Risk Management Techniques"."

The Ultimate Advantage

The aim is to provide value to your readers, making them see the practical applications and importance of risk management, thereby establishing your business as an authoritative voice in the domain.

Best Practices for Engaging Content:

Visual Aids: Incorporate infographics, charts, or short videos to make your posts more engaging and easier to comprehend. A visual representation of risk assessment metrics or a quick animated video on the latest risk management tools can enhance user engagement manifold.

User Engagement: Encourage users to share their experiences or thoughts. After sharing a post on regulatory changes, you could ask, "How do you think this will impact the small businesses in the sector? Share your thoughts below!"."

Use Relevant Hashtags: Appropriate hashtags increase the visibility of your posts. For instance, using #RiskManagementUpdates, #IndustryInsights, or #RegulatoryNews can help reach a broader audience looking for this specific information.

Stay Updated with Trends: Platforms like Twitter often have trending topics. If there's a trending topic relevant to risk management, engage in that conversation to increase visibility.

Interactive Content: Polls or quizzes related to risk management can be an interactive way to engage users. A poll like "Which risk management tool do you find most effective? A) Tool X, B) Tool Y, C) Tool Z" can stimulate interaction and also provide insights into client preferences.

Engaging your clients on social media isn't just about posting content; it's about posting the right content that resonates with them and offers tangible value. By sharing insights and writing in-depth blogs, not only do you position yourself as an authority in risk management, but you also build trust with your audience, which is invaluable in the long run.

Calendar Integration

In today's fast-paced business landscape, commercial insurance agents must prioritize ease of access to stay competitive and cater to the ever-evolving needs of clients. Being readily available for your clients can indeed be the difference between gaining a loyal customer and losing a potential business opportunity. There are two game-changing strategies that insurance agents should consider implementing to amplify their accessibility:

Self-Service Scheduling:

One of the most tangible ways to enhance accessibility is by implementing self-service scheduling tools, like Calendly or Acuity. These tools are revolutionizing the way businesses operate and engage with clients. They allow clients and prospects to autonomously book appointments, saving both parties significant time and effort.

Picture this: A business owner is shopping for commercial insurance. It's late at night, and they're doing their research. They stumble upon your services and are impressed. They want to schedule a consultation. If they have to wait until morning to send an email, wait for a response, and then coordinate a time that works for both parties, the momentum is lost. They might even explore your competitors' websites in the meantime. But with tools like Calendly, they can instantly book a slot that works for both parties, right when their interest is at its peak.

The Ultimate Advantage

The elimination of the traditional back-and-forth emailing not only saves time but also enhances the client's experience by offering them immediate action. They feel more in control, and the ease of the process leaves a lasting positive impression.

Sync across Devices:

With the rise of technology and various devices at our disposal, it's paramount that commercial insurance agents utilize systems that sync in real-time across all gadgets. Be it your desktop, tablet, or smartphone, real-time syncing ensures that you're always in the loop regarding your appointments. This eradicates the chances of double bookings, missing an appointment, or being caught off-guard.

Let's say you're at a networking event, and someone expresses interest in your services. You quickly check your availability on your smartphone and lock in a meeting. Real-time syncing ensures that this new entry reflects instantly across all your devices, minimizing the risk of oversights.

For commercial insurance agents aiming for growth and excellent client service, integrating these ease-of-access tools and strategies is not just recommended; it's essential. They not only streamline operations but also significantly improve client satisfaction and trust. And in the world of insurance, where relationships and trust are paramount, these tools can be the key to unlocking unparalleled success.

Video Conferencing Software

For commercial insurance agents operating in a rapidly digitizing world, the conventional understanding of "transportation" has transformed. Traditionally, transportation meant physically moving from one place to another. However, with the proliferation of digital technologies, transportation now also encompasses the ability to transport oneself into a virtual space, connecting people instantaneously irrespective of geographical boundaries.

Reconceptualizing Transportation in the Digital Age:

When we ponder transportation technologies, our immediate thoughts veer towards vehicles, roads, and the infrastructure that facilitates physical mobility. However, in today's age, where digital connectivity outpaces physical connections, platforms like Zoom and Microsoft Teams are emerging as the new-age "transportation technologies"." These platforms swiftly "transport" professionals into meetings and discussions irrespective of where they or their clients are located in the world.

Virtual Face-to-Face Meetings:

In an industry like commercial insurance, where relationship building is paramount, face-to-face meetings have always held a significant place. While physical meetings have their undeniable charm, the power of virtual meetings cannot be ignored. With platforms like Zoom and Microsoft Teams, agents can host virtual face-to-face meetings that allow for personal interactions without the constraints of location. This immediacy not only saves time but also minimizes logistical challenges.

Moreover, in a world witnessing a surge in non-standard employment structures and remote work, these platforms ensure that commercial insurance agents remain agile and responsive to client needs.

Webinars as a Tool for Engagement:

The Ultimate Advantage

Beyond one-on-one meetings, digital platforms enable commercial insurance agents to host webinars. This format serves as a powerful tool to disseminate information on insurance topics, regulations, and industry best practices. Webinars offer a two-fold advantage: they position agents as industry thought leaders and serve as an effective platform to engage both existing clients and prospects.

In a study on digital globalization, it was noted that the flow of information across borders has witnessed an explosive growth, primarily driven by digital communication and platforms that enable real-time sharing of knowledge. Webinars, thus, become a strategic tool in a commercial insurance agent's arsenal to tap into this flow and cater to a global audience.

Implications for the Insurance Industry:

As the insurance industry grapples with the challenges and opportunities presented by AI and digital transformation, the role of digital communication platforms as transportation tools gains even more prominence. Agents are not just competing with local peers but are part of a global marketplace where clients have access to international players.

In such a scenario, the ability to "transport" oneself into any meeting across the globe, engage in virtual yet personal discussions, and offer real-time insights becomes a significant differentiator.

Preparing for the Future:

As the lines between physical and digital blur, commercial insurance agents must equip themselves with the skills to navigate these digital platforms efficiently. Embracing this new form of "transportation technology" requires a shift in mindset – understanding that being present digitally can sometimes be as impactful, if not more, than being present physically.

Future technological trends suggest a further intertwining of our digital and physical realities, and these platforms will undoubtedly play an even more critical role.

For commercial insurance agents, platforms like Zoom and Microsoft Teams represent more than just communication tools. They are the new-age transportation technologies, bridging geographical gaps, and ensuring that agents remain at the forefront of client engagement in a digitally connected world. Embracing these platforms while understanding their transformative nature is the way forward for agents who want to thrive in this digital age.

AI Assistance

In today's dynamic and rapidly changing world, the insurance industry faces an ever-evolving landscape of challenges and opportunities. With advancements in Artificial Intelligence (AI), commercial agents now have a powerful ally to assist them in selling more insurance. Through AI, agents can revolutionize their marketing strategies, optimize the sales process, and uncover novel ways to identify prospects and convert them into loyal clients.

Streamlining the Sales Process with AI: At the heart of any sales venture is the process. Traditional methods, although tried and tested, often come with inefficiencies. AI can automate routine tasks, ensuring agents spend more time selling and less time on administrative duties. For instance, AI can automate follow-up emails or reminders, ensuring potential leads are nurtured without manual intervention.

AI-Enhanced Email Campaigns: One of the primary touchpoints for agents with prospects is email. Through AI, email content can be optimized based on the recipient's preferences and past interactions. For example, if a prospect had previously shown interest in commercial property insurance, AI can tailor the email content to highlight testimonials from similar businesses or case studies, making the proposition more relatable and compelling.

Finding Answers to Complex Queries: AI can assist agents in providing instant responses to client's queries. With the integration of AI, an agent's system can instantly fetch data, insights, or research to answer complex questions, ensuring the agent is always prepared and appears knowledgeable, thus building trust.

Discovering New Avenues for Prospects: AI can analyze vast amounts of data to identify potential markets or niches that agents might not have considered. By analyzing market trends, social media behaviors, and more, AI can suggest areas where there's a demand for specific insurance products, enabling agents to target their efforts more effectively.

Optimizing Marketing Strategies with AI: Gone are the days when agents relied solely on traditional advertising. With AI, agents can develop dynamic marketing strategies, adjusting in real-time based on the audience's response. For instance, if an online ad campaign for a specific insurance product isn't resonating with the target demographic, AI can immediately tweak the messaging or visuals, ensuring optimal engagement.

Personalized Client Experiences: Personalization is no longer a luxury but a necessity in sales. AI can analyze a client's or prospect's data to offer tailored recommendations. Imagine an agent approaching a business that recently expanded its operations overseas. AI could prompt the agent to discuss relevant international commercial policies, making the pitch more relevant and timelier.

Lead Scoring and Prioritization: Not all leads are created equal. AI can analyze the behavior, interaction history, and other parameters of prospects to score and rank them. Agents can then prioritize their efforts, focusing on leads that have a higher likelihood of conversion, ensuring a better return on investment.

Chatbots for Preliminary Engagement: While chatbots are often associated with customer service, they have a crucial role in the initial sales process. Chatbots can engage with website visitors, answer basic queries, and even set up appointments with agents. This ensures that when the agent interacts with the prospect, they already have a foundation to build upon.

AI-Driven Content Creation for Marketing: AI tools today can generate content, be it blog posts, social media updates, or articles, tailored to resonate with the target audience. This ensures that the agent's marketing efforts are always fresh, relevant, and engaging.

Feedback Analysis for Continuous Improvement: After interactions, AI can analyze feedback to help agents refine their approach and tactics. By leveraging AI, these evaluations can be done in real-time, allowing agents to adjust strategies instantly based on client feedback. This not only ensures continuous improvement but also fosters trust with clients as they see agents being proactive and responsive.

Network Building through AI: Modern AI-driven platforms can analyze various data sources to identify potential referral opportunities or partnerships. Agents can be notified about businesses or individuals within their clients' networks who might be looking for insurance products, thus expanding their potential client base organically.

Predictive Analysis for Market Trends: AI tools equipped with predictive analytics can forecast market trends, allowing agents to adapt their product offerings and marketing strategies accordingly. For example, if AI identifies an upcoming surge in demand for cyber liability insurance due to increased cyber threats, agents can proactively market this product to businesses.

Enhancing Client Retention through Proactive Services: AI can assist agents in monitoring clients' changing circumstances, flagging potential areas where additional insurance coverage might be needed. This proactive approach can enhance client loyalty, as it shows the agent's genuine concern and proactive approach towards their clients' well-being.

Educative Content Generation: AI tools can also generate educative content relevant to current market situations, which agents can share with their clients. This positions the agent as a trusted advisor rather than just a salesperson, deepening the client-agent relationship.

By embracing the capabilities of AI, commercial agents can transcend traditional barriers, reinvent their sales processes, and engage more meaningfully with their prospects and clients. This not only ensures increased sales but also fosters stronger, lasting relationships in the competitive insurance landscape.

Embracing technology is not about replacing the human touch that's integral to insurance dealings; it's about augmenting it. When agents merge their industry expertise with the power of these tools, they can offer unparalleled service, optimize their operations, and stand out in a competitive market. The future of commercial insurance is bright, and with the right technological allies, agents are well-equipped to shine.

Chapter 16 The Relationship between Underwriters and Commercial Insurance Salespeople

The insurance industry, vast and complex, operates on the collective efforts of many. Two crucial roles underpinning the entire structure are those of underwriters and insurance salespeople or agents. These roles are not only interdependent but also central to the smooth functioning of the insurance mechanism. Let's delve deeper into the significance of their relationship and how their dynamics shape the world of insurance.

Underwriters and Insurance Salespeople: The Symbiotic Relationship

Underwriters and insurance agents, though performing different functions, come together to form a harmonious relationship that defines the core of insurance transactions. Agents are on the frontline, working with potential policyholders, understanding their needs, and gathering critical information. They focus on building relationships, acquiring clients, and understanding the intricacies of clients' demands and risk factors. Their efforts culminate in the acquisition of policies, ensuring the right coverages are set in place for each client.

Contrarily, underwriters operate behind the scenes, meticulously analyzing risks associated with potential clients. Using data and analytical tools, they determine if the insurance company should take on the risk and, if so, under what terms and pricing. Their decisions are fundamental; a single misjudgment can result in significant financial setbacks for insurance companies. This immense responsibility demands precision, expertise, and sound judgment.

The relationship between agents and underwriters is a symbiotic one. Agents provide the relevant information and context about the potential policyholder, and underwriters determine the viability of insuring these clients, finalizing the terms of coverage.

Underwriters and Profitable Growth

Interestingly, underwriters are often incentivized based on the profitability of the policies they underwrite. Bonuses and other financial incentives are commonly tied to profitable growth. This structure ensures that underwriters remain vigilant, prioritizing policies that not only add to the volume of business but also bring in profitable returns.

This profitability factor suggests a clear direction for agents: to focus on bringing underwriters prospects that align with the goal of profitable growth. By ensuring that the risk profiles of clients are favorable, agents can support underwriters in their pursuit of achieving targeted profitability.

The Broker of Record (BOR)

Securing the Broker of Record (BOR) gives agents control over the account. This move often signifies a shift in agency or a reevaluation of terms. When an underwriter receives a submission with the BOR, there's an added layer of excitement and seriousness. They recognize this as a genuine opportunity, not just a casual inquiry. It represents potential business, a real chance at profitable growth, and an earnest effort from the agent's side.

The Communication Gap: A Perennial Issue

A recurring challenge in the insurance industry is the perceived communication gap between agents and underwriters. Often, agents, in their rush or due to oversight, provide minimal or inadequate information. Underwriters, working with incomplete data, find it challenging to make informed decisions, leading to delays or unfavorable terms. The lament of underwriters is clear: agents sometimes make their job harder than it should be.

Conversely, agents often complain about underwriters being overly cautious or conservative, avoiding taking on risks, even when they seem manageable from the agent's perspective. The sentiment among some agents is that underwriters are hesitant to write policies.

However, the solution to this perennial problem is straightforward: communication and consistency. Agents who have a history of consistently providing comprehensive, accurate, and clear submissions invariably find it easier to work with underwriters. They establish a reputation of reliability, making underwriters more confident in their submissions and more willing to write policies based on the information provided. In essence, a perfect submission is not just about the present transaction; it's about building a lasting, productive relationship.

By understanding each other's roles, challenges, and objectives, and by communicating effectively, these two pillars can work harmoniously, driving the industry forward and ensuring clients receive the best possible coverage.

Crafting the Perfect Submission

The Narrative:

The narrative serves as a holistic portrait of the client, enabling underwriters to grasp the nuances of the client's profile. A well-constructed narrative delves into the intricacies of a client's business model, organizational history, management structures, and even their projected growth or strategic pivots. The objective is to paint a picture that's detailed enough to capture the essence of the client's operations and potential associated risks, giving the underwriter the tools they need to evaluate the proposal. This is the most important part of the submission and must be completed by the producer. You must convey to the underwriter WHY you are writing this account. Include how you met the client and whether you have already received the BOR on this account. This is also where you describe why this is a good risk for the carrier. Anything in the loss runs should also be explained here including what steps the client has taken to mediate any future event. I like to include the clients' plans for future growth and current success. This is also where you let the underwriter know what pricing and terms you are expecting to close this deal and any other pertinent coverages needed.

Accords:

ACCORD forms are pivotal to the insurance industry as standardized templates for collecting client-specific information. Every data point captured in these forms plays a role in the underwriting process, making accuracy and completeness paramount. If there are special circumstances or unique data points about the client that can't be encapsulated within the form's standard fields, agents should include an explanatory note or annex, providing the underwriter with the full context.

Loss Runs:

Think of loss runs as a client's risk report card. These documents catalog the history of claims made by a client over a typical period of three to five years. By reviewing these reports, underwriters can gauge past risk patterns and make educated guesses about future vulnerabilities. An up-to-date loss run is invaluable as it gives an unfiltered view of the client's risk management practices and potential pitfalls.

1. **Photos**:

    Visuals serve as an instant gateway to understanding assets or potential risk areas. Whether it's a property, equipment, or any other tangible asset, photographs can highlight conditions, maintenance levels, and even operational practices. For maximum utility, each photo should be high quality, stamped with a date, and labeled clearly to identify what it represents. This tangible proof often helps underwriters in corroborating the details presented in the narrative and other accompanying documents.

    Additional Documents:

    Insurance is not a one-size-fits-all industry, and depending on the specific coverage being sought, different supplemental documents might be essential. For instance, if a business seeks coverage for workplace injuries, they may need to provide details about their safety protocols and employee training regimes. For financial-based insurances, like Directors and Officers insurance, up-to-date financial statements can be paramount. Agents should always be proactive in understanding the unique documentation needs of their client's sought coverage and ensure all pertinent documents are submitted in the package.

    In essence, crafting the perfect submission revolves around communication, clarity, and comprehensiveness. The goal is to preemptively answer any questions the underwriter might have, smoothing the pathway to an efficient and effective underwriting process. This is an example of an email to an underwriter about an account.

    Dear [Underwriter's Name],

The Ultimate Advantage

I am writing to present a comprehensive portrait of our valued client, OilTech Precision Manufacturing. As a seasoned insurance producer, I've had the privilege of representing various manufacturing companies, but OilTech's dedication and robust infrastructure particularly stand out. I met the CEO Mr. Alan Smith at the annual oil producers conference last summer. Over the last few months, I have had several in person and virtual visits with Mr. Smith and his staff and I am pleased to let you know we have secured a BOR for all his policies. I am attaching the letter with this submission. You are not currently on this account but based on my knowledge of the types of risks you are looking for and my knowledge of this account I wanted to present this to you first.

Company History: Established in 1980, OilTech Precision Manufacturing has carved its niche in crafting high-grade parts vital for the oil and gas industry. Their dedication to quality has garnered them partnerships with leading industry players over four decades.

Previous Loss Explanation: In 2019, a supply chain disruption led to an unforeseen loss. Promptly addressing this, OilTech implemented tighter supply chain management protocols and partnered with diverse suppliers to avert such incidents in the future.

Future Projections: OilTech has laid out a strategic plan focusing on R&D, aiming to innovate and cater to the evolving needs of the oil and gas sector. They anticipate a 15% annual growth for the next five years, emphasizing sustainability and eco-friendly manufacturing.

Executive Staff Bios:

- Mr. Alan Smith, CEO: A petroleum engineer with twenty-five years in the oil and gas industry. His visionary leadership has been pivotal for OilTech.

The Ultimate Advantage

- Ms. Lydia Clarke, CFO: With a stellar track record in corporate finance, Lydia's fiscal strategies have ensured consistent profitability.

- Mr. Jacob Fields, COO: Jacob's operational expertise has streamlined production, reducing costs while elevating quality.

I believe OilTech Precision Manufacturing embodies a promising and low-risk proposition. Their proactive management, robust business model, and future-oriented strategies make them an ideal candidate for underwriting. The expiring premium on _____ is xxxxx we would like to see yyyyyy for this term based on OilTech's increased performance year after year.

Thank you for considering our submission and I look forward to speaking with you about this account.

Warm regards,

John's Story: His Heroic Journey as a New Commercial Insurance Producer

The Ultimate Advantage

We embark on a transformative journey alongside our protagonist, John. From the humble beginnings of curiosity and ambition, we watch as he navigates the labyrinth of the commercial world, facing challenges, forging relationships, and ultimately carving out his niche as a commercial agent. John's path, though fictional, serves as an embodiment of the principles, insights, and lessons encapsulated in the preceding chapters of this book. As we follow his story, readers are not merely observing as his tale unfolds; they are witnessing the practical application of the book's teachings. The narrative bridges theory with reality, allowing us to see how the abstract concepts discussed come to life in the real-world decisions and actions of our hero. It is a tale of triumph, perseverance, and the relentless pursuit of one's goals, all set against the backdrop of the intricate and ever-evolving world of commerce. Join John, and let's see how the lessons we've learned play out in his odyssey.

The Ordinary World

John had recently secured a position at Stratton Insurance, a well-regarded local agency that specialized in commercial insurance. The air was thick with the scent of coffee and the low murmur of phone conversations as he walked through the open-concept office on his first day. It was a place where everyone knew your name, and there was a sense of camaraderie that was immediately palpable.

"Welcome to the team, John," greeted Kathy, the agency's Vice President, offering a firm handshake. "We have high hopes for you."

The Ultimate Advantage

"Thank you, Kathy. I'm really excited to be here," John replied, a mix of anticipation and nerves in his voice.

After some initial introductions and a quick tour of the office, John found himself in the orientation room with Robert, the agency's Senior Producer and mentor for new hires. Robert was a seasoned professional, the kind of guy whose stories from the field could fill books.

"Alright, kid, first things first. You're licensed, right?" Robert asked as he swiveled around in his chair to face John.

"Yes, sir. Just it last month," John affirmed.

"Good. Now, let's talk about your compensation model. You'll be working on a base salary plus commission. The more you sell, the more you make. Sound fair?" Robert continued.

"Absolutely, sounds motivating," John responded, already mentally calculating the opportunities.

"That's the spirit! But remember, it's not just about selling; it's about selling the right products to the right clients. It's a nuanced game," Robert added.

Robert then introduced John to some of his new colleagues. "This is Scott, he's your go-to for anything related to underwriting. And that's Emily; she's a wizard with customer relations. You'll learn a lot from them."

"Nice to meet you all. I look forward to working with you," John said, shaking hands with each of them.

"Likewise," Scott responded. "We were all newbies once. Don't hesitate to ask questions."

"Absolutely, always happy to help," Emily added with a smile.

As John settled into his new workspace, armed with the standard office supplies, his walls and shelves an empty canvas waiting to be filled with photos and awards celebrating his accomplishments, he couldn't help but feel a mixture of exhilaration and apprehension. There was a lot to learn, from mastering the intricacies of various insurance products to understanding the nuances of fulfilling customer needs. He knew he had a steep learning curve ahead but was equally aware of the rewarding journey that awaited him.

His first assignment was to identify a niche he wanted to focus on, a critical first step in narrowing down his prospective client list. John felt a bit overwhelmed. There were so many sectors, each with its unique challenges and needs. How could he choose?

Sensing his hesitation, Robert walked over to his desk. "Hey, you look a bit lost. First-day jitters?"

"Yeah, a bit," John admitted. "I'm just not sure which niche to focus on."

"Don't worry; it's a common dilemma," Robert assured him. "Just remember, choose a sector you're passionate about. Your enthusiasm will shine through when you're talking to prospects. It makes a world of difference."

That evening, John found himself going through the chapters of the book *The Ultimate Advantage* that had initially inspired him to pursue this career. Each chapter, each principle seemed to be speaking directly to him, reminding him of the roadmap he had for his journey. He remembered the emphasis on identifying a niche, the importance of ethical selling, and the need for continuous learning. Each point was a nudge, guiding him on the path he had chosen. He felt a newfound sense of clarity. Drawing on the knowledge he gained from the book to keep him

The Ultimate Advantage

motivated he imagined the author cheering him on with the words, "You've got this."

As John closed the book and reflected on his day, he felt a combination of fatigue and excitement. The path ahead was long, filled with challenges he couldn't yet foresee. But John also felt equipped, supported by a team that was willing to guide him, and armed with principles that would serve as his compass. He knew he was just at the beginning, and the real work was still to come, but he felt ready. More than anything, he knew that this was a journey worth embarking on.

John felt a sense of accomplishment as he walked into Robert's office. After weeks of researching, he had finally pinpointed two niches that he was excited to specialize in: local restaurants and data center operations. He couldn't wait to get Robert's feedback.

"Hey, Robert. Do you have a minute? I think I've found the niches I want to focus on," John announced, a glint of excitement in his eyes.

Robert looked up from his laptop and gestured for John to take a seat. "Absolutely, let's hear it."

"I'm thinking of specializing in local restaurants and data center operations. They both seem interesting and diverse enough for me to build my portfolio around them," John laid out his vision confidently.

Robert steepled his fingers and leaned back in his chair, pondering for a moment. "Interesting choices. But before we get ahead of ourselves, have you considered the average revenue per client in these markets?"

John's enthusiasm dimmed a bit. "Well, not in detail, but I figured local restaurants are everywhere, and data centers are crucial in this digital age."

Robert sighed, "John, this is the part where we have to marry passion with practicality. Let's break down the categories for our agency's revenue per client. Anything under $1,500 is considered 'small,' and anything over $10,000 is "middle." The 'schmiddle' is in between, from $1,500 to $10,000. Our sweet spot, however, is around $5,000. That's where we hit the goldilocks zone of not much competition from smaller agencies but still allowing us to offer something that the large national brokers often overlook."

"I see," John muttered, realizing the depth of his oversight.

Robert continued, "Local restaurants, while numerous, tend to fall into the 'small' to 'schmiddle' category. Data centers, on the other hand, can easily be middle-market accounts, given the multiple insurances they'll require—cybersecurity, property, business interruption, and so on."

"But why is the $5,000 revenue range so special?" John asked.

Robert smiled, "Great question. You see, at that level, companies are just starting to get complicated enough to require a risk advisor, not just an insurance salesman. They need the kind of in-depth service that we specialize in."

"Okay, I'm beginning to understand the strategy," John nodded.

"Let me share the story of Anthony," Robert said, leaning forward. "He's been with us for over twenty years. When he started, he was ecstatic about local restaurants and dentist's offices. He loved the social aspect of it. And you know what? He hardly ever met his revenue goals. He's only hit it twice in two decades!"

John's eyes widened. "Really? But he's such a seasoned producer!"

"Seasoned, yes. But a top risk advisor? Far from it," Robert quipped. "Look, he's got the cleanest teeth and has eaten at every local joint you can think of, but after twenty years, it's a lesson learned the hard way. He shifted his focus to larger property accounts just five years ago and that's when he started to see real success."

"That's an eye-opener," John admitted.

Robert leaned in, "John, I'd hate for you to repeat history. Sure, local restaurants may be a fun sector, but if you're going to build a career, you should aim for sectors that not only interest you but also meet our revenue targets. You have to set the stage now, or else you'll end up like Anthony—lots of fun experiences, but not much to show for it in your career."

John felt as if he had dodged a bullet. His initial excitement about diving headfirst into his niches now seemed naïve. "So, I go back to the drawing board?"

"Not necessarily," Robert offered, "you could still keep local restaurants as a 'hobby niche' but focus more on data centers. Alternatively, find another middle-market niche that excites you as much as data centers do."

With a deep sense of gratitude, John thanked Robert and left his office. The corridor seemed longer than usual as he made his way back to his desk, his mind racing with new ideas and perspectives. It was clear now; he had to realign his plans with the agency's focus if he was going to build a long-lasting, rewarding career.

His earlier vision was not entirely wrong, just incomplete. It lacked the strategic depth that considered average revenue per client, competition, and the ever-crucial sweet spot for the agency. But now, with Robert's insights and Anthony's cautionary tale in mind, John was ready to refine his approach. Data centers were definitely staying on his list. As for the second niche, he thought about green technology companies—a sector that fascinated him and was likely to fall into the middle-market segment.

Sitting back at his desk, John felt more confident than ever. The road ahead was challenging, but he now had a map. And on this journey, he wouldn't just find clients; he'd discover his own capacity for strategic thinking, relationship-building, and ultimately, success. Gone were the days of choosing niches based on mere surface-level appeal. Now he had the tools to analyze, adapt, and pursue sectors that would not just pique his interest but would also set him on the path to long-term success.

John sat alone at his desk, staring at his computer screen, which was just as blank as his client list. Despite the enthusiasm that came with identifying his niche, the following weeks proved overwhelming. He had meticulously put together a list of potential clients—owners of local gyms and high-end artisanal shops, believing he was on the right track in his focus on companies that could create a lucrative stream of business.

He had sent out targeted email campaigns highlighting the risks that business owners like them often overlooked, and how he could offer tailored insurance solutions. He had put in hours crafting content that he thought would be both engaging and informative. But what he got in return was a deafening silence.

The Ultimate Advantage

Rejection is never easy, but for John, it was disheartening on a level he had never experienced. He had prepared himself for the occasional nos, but he wasn't prepared for utter indifference. The deafening silence from potential clients was like a mirror reflecting his deepest insecurities. Each ignored email and overlooked marketing campaign left him questioning not just his professional skills but his entire decision to become a commercial insurance producer.

There were days when John couldn't even summon the energy to get out of bed. The thought of facing another day of unreturned emails and cold calls that went nowhere was enough to send him diving back under the covers. His relationship began to suffer too; he lied to his girlfriend Carmen, saying he was off to meetings when he would just drive around town aimlessly, feeling completely defeated. He couldn't bear to tell her that he was failing at the one job he thought he would excel in.

His mentor Robert, who usually had an uplifting piece of advice, was out of state on a sixty-day vacation. In Robert's absence, John had brief conversations with Anthony, another senior producer at the agency. Anthony had been in the industry for twenty years but his perspective was not what John had hoped for.

"This industry isn't for everyone, kid," Anthony had said, looking at John's desolate client list. "Maybe you need a business coach. Or perhaps you should start smaller—lower your goals like I did. I focused on dentist's offices and restaurants when I started. Granted, it took me a long time to make anything out of it, but here I am."

Although Anthony meant well, his advice did little to lift John's spirits. It made him feel like he was already a lost cause, someone who had to adjust his ambitions because he didn't have what it takes to achieve them.

The Ultimate Advantage

Kathy, the agency's Vice President, was also concerned but for a different reason. "You're not setting enough meetings," she said in passing, seemingly oblivious to the turmoil John was experiencing. "In our line of work, it's all about numbers. You've got to hustle more."

Her words, intended to be constructive, felt like another nail in his confidence's coffin. Hustle more? He was already struggling to get even a single lead.

Feeling defeated, John seriously contemplated quitting. Maybe insurance just wasn't his field. Maybe he should go back to school or find another job where the bar was lower, where expectations were less demanding. And yet, despite the allure of these thoughts, John remembered the excitement he felt when he first landed the job. He thought of the countless hours he spent studying and getting licensed, his dreams of helping businesses manage risks effectively, of becoming a top producer at his agency, and eventually, in the industry.

It was a dream he still wasn't ready to give up on, no matter how difficult the path seemed at the moment. But dreams wouldn't pay his bills or silence his self-doubt. He knew he needed to do something different, something drastic. But what? He had followed every piece of advice he had received, checked every box he thought was important, and yet here he was, with nothing to show for his efforts.

As he pondered his future, John realized he had reached a pivotal moment in his life. He could continue to drown in self-doubt, or he could swim against the tide, no matter how strong it was. While he still didn't have all the answers, he knew one thing for sure: it was high time for a change, a substantial one. And even though his mentor was away and his colleagues' advice had been less than inspiring, he knew the real change had to come from within him. Robert would be back in two months, and when he did return, John

The Ultimate Advantage

wanted to have a different story to tell, a story not of defeat but of resilience and hopefully, success.

He sat back down at his desk, erased his old client list, and started anew, vowing to himself that he wouldn't give up, not yet. He might be down, but he wasn't out, and sometimes, that's all that mattered.

In the midst of his struggle, a glimmer of hope appeared in John's life when he registered for a BIG I event, a must-attend for insurance professionals. That was where he crossed paths with Mark, a seasoned veteran in the insurance world who had managed, owned, and recently sold his own successful agency. Mark was leading a breakout session on sales strategies, and John, hungry for any insights that could turn his fledgling career around, eagerly took a seat.

Mark was an engaging speaker. He talked about a range of topics, from time management skills to intricate sales techniques. What really caught John's attention, however, was the concept of "Hacking" time management by batching and blocking tasks. The idea seemed revolutionary to John, who often found himself bogged down with a dozen tasks that ate into his productive hours.

Mark went on to introduce the Eisenhower Box, a simple decision-making tool that helps prioritize tasks based on their urgency and importance. He explained that one's ability to decide what is crucial and what can wait is often the key to a successful career. But Mark didn't stop there. He also introduced the Pomodoro Technique as a method for boosting focus and productivity. The idea was to work in short, intensely focused bursts, followed by brief breaks to relax and recharge.

After the session, intrigued and inspired, John decided to approach Mark. There was a crowd around him, each person eager to have a one-on-one moment, but John patiently waited. When it was finally his turn, he said, "Your session was incredibly enlightening, Mark. I've been struggling a lot lately as a new producer, and your advice seems like it could really help."

Mark looked at John for a moment before responding, "Well, the first step to improving is knowing that you need to improve. So, you're already on the right path."

Something about John's earnestness and humility struck a chord with Mark. He had seen countless young, eager faces come and go in this industry. Some burned out quickly, overwhelmed by the complexity and pace, while others became jaded, settling into a habit of doing a mediocre job. But there was a quality in John—a sort of resilient curiosity—that made him think he just might be different.

"Listen," Mark said, "I don't know what specifically you're struggling with, but let me tell you this: the principles you read in that book *The Ultimate Advantage*. You mentioned they are your anchor. You need to fine-tune your strategies continually, and more importantly, you must stick with it. This industry rewards persistence and penalizes hesitation."

John listened intently, absorbing every word. Here was a man who had weathered the storms that John was currently navigating, and he was willing to offer guidance.

"I've been there," Mark continued. "I've had my share of days when it felt like the phone weighed a thousand pounds, when the last thing I wanted to do was make another cold call or face another rejection. But I stuck with it. I revisited my strategies, adjusted my sails, and powered through. And look where it got me."

It was as if a fog had lifted. John felt like he was seeing things clearly for the first time in weeks. "Thank you, Mark. Really, I can't tell you how much this means to me."

The Ultimate Advantage

"Don't thank me yet," Mark smiled. "Thank me when you've turned your career around and you're the one standing here, imparting wisdom to the next generation."

As they parted ways, John felt a renewed sense of purpose. Mark's words had struck a chord deep within him. He realized that no book or course could replace the value of hard-earned experience and wisdom from someone who had walked the path he aspired to traverse.

Returning to his desk the next day, the Eisenhower Box on one side and a Pomodoro timer on the other, John felt different, empowered, focused, and more importantly, hopeful. It was like he had been given a second chance, and he was determined not to waste it. With Mark's teachings in mind, he started re-strategizing his approach, fine-tuning his methods, and most importantly, persisting despite the obstacles.

For the first time in a long time, John felt like success was not just a distant dream but an achievable reality. His journey had been fraught with challenges and self-doubt, but meeting Mark made him believe that the road ahead, while not easy, was certainly navigable.

With this newfound perspective, he understood that his failures were not roadblocks but steppingstones on his path to success. Mark had rekindled the flame within him, and this time, John was not going to let it go out.

The road had been tough for John, but the mentorship he received from Mark proved to be a turning point in his journey as a commercial insurance producer. His workspace, once a chaotic mix of tasks and half-formed ideas, was now organized and filled with energy. John now had systems in place—tools and strategies he'd learned from Mark that had elevated his approach from haphazard to highly strategic.

It wasn't just about the Eisenhower Box or the Pomodoro Technique; it was about an entire philosophy of consistent learning and adaptability. Based on Mark's advice, John revisited the book he had initially read when he entered the industry and found a chapter on continuous learning especially resonant this time. Mark even encouraged him to deepen his knowledge by pursuing various designations from esteemed organizations such as the National Alliance, the Institutes, and RIMS. Taking this to heart, John enrolled in an online CIC (Certified Insurance Counselor) course, ready to bring more expertise to his client relationships.

His marketing approach also underwent a revolutionary change. Gone were the generic, template-based emails he used to send out in desperation. In their place were personalized messages that showcased his deep understanding of each prospect's needs. He focused on providing value upfront—a key takeaway from Mark's teachings—and his emails started getting responses.

Beyond email outreach, John took another step-in market engagement. He began attending tech meetups, where he could mingle with entrepreneurs and decision-makers in the booming tech sector. It was at one such meetup that he got his first real break—a meeting with a green energy company specializing in the manufacturing and installation of wind turbines and solar panels on commercial buildings. They were scaling up quickly and needed a skilled insurance advisor. For John, the alignment couldn't have been more perfect.

Adding to this, John had been diligent in leveraging his agency's CRM software to fine-tune his messaging. His marketing campaigns were now more focused, targeting specific client pain points and offering tangible solutions. He started winning business—writing policies for local restaurants that he and his girlfriend Carmen loved to visit.

During dinner one evening, John looked across the table at Carmen, his eyes alight with excitement and conviction. "Carmen," he began, "I've never been more committed to my career than I am now. The advice and strategies I've picked up from Mark have made a world of difference. I'm not just scraping the bottom anymore; I'm growing, and you know what the best part is? This is only the beginning."

Carmen could see the change in him—the gleam in his eyes, the newfound confidence, and the excitement that had replaced the weariness he'd been carrying around for weeks. "I'm proud of you, John," she said, her voice tinged with emotion. "I always knew you had it in you. The future is wide open for us."

Indeed, John felt that the future was not just an abstract concept anymore. It was a tangible, reachable thing, filled with opportunities he was now equipped to grasp. His phone, which had once felt like a thousand-pound weight, now represented a gateway to endless possibilities. With Mark's wisdom still echoing in his ears and a newfound momentum, John was crossing a significant threshold. Not only was he excited about the immediate opportunities, like the green energy company, but he was also thrilled about what lay further down the road.

Mark continued to check in with him every few weeks, reinforcing that the road to mastery is a continuous one. His mentorship was a steady compass in John's evolving journey, a journey that was becoming less about struggling to survive and more about scaling new heights.

As he sat there, enjoying dinner with Carmen, John felt like he was stepping into a new chapter, one filled with promise

The Ultimate Advantage

and potential. And for the first time in his life, he felt ready to turn the page.

John was gradually settling into the rhythm of his new career, enjoying small victories that were lighting up his path like fireflies on a dark night. Responses started trickling in after the slew of emails he sent out, appointments started materializing on his calendar, and his first deals were inked, though modest. He was, as the saying goes, on his way.

His work with Green Revolution—a green energy firm spearheaded by Kevin Wright; a former Green Beret turned entrepreneur—had been progressing smoothly. The initial meeting had gone exceptionally well, a combination of mutual respect and shared values that seemed to promise a fruitful partnership. Kevin had made it clear that he wasn't pleased with his current insurance set-up; the previous agent was a family friend who had recently retired, and Kevin suspected that he had never fully understood the intricacies of the green energy sector. With Kevin's keen interest in working with someone more aligned with his vision, John felt poised to present a conceptual proposal in the coming weeks.

Back in the office, John ran into Kathy, the Vice President, who commended him on his burgeoning success. Eager to share, John told her about his meeting with Kevin and how much he looked forward to deepening this relationship. Kathy's response was cautionary.

"John, it's great to hear that you're making progress. But you should know what you're up against," Sarah began. "Karen is an agent with a large national insurance firm, known for her vast portfolio of green energy business clients. She's going to be tough competition. Her firm has significant resources, and she's known for playing hardball."

His mentor Robert, who had recently returned from his vacation, had more to add when John brought up Karen's name later. Robert's expression darkened noticeably. "Karen is... how do I put this politely? She's the sort of agent who will use every tool at her disposal to win. She leverages the sheer size of her agency to outperform and overshadow smaller competitors like us."

Robert continued, "I want you to remember the chapter on reputation in that book you read. Reputation isn't just about what people say about you; it's also about the company you keep. Karen has left a trail of burned bridges behind her—relationships with other agents, underwriters, and even clients. Her tactics border on the unethical, and she often Comes off as entitled."

John felt a twinge of apprehension, but also a spark of competitive spirit. If Karen was as cutthroat as Robert described, then he would need to be on his A-game. Tom's advice on focusing on building his reputation lingered in his mind. He knew that ethical conduct and genuinely good work would be his greatest allies in this high-stakes power play.

But it wasn't just about outmaneuvering Karen or impressing Robert. John understood that this was a test of his abilities, a chance to demonstrate the skills he had honed, the wisdom he had gathered from Mark, and the industry knowledge he was acquiring through his ongoing education. It was a challenge he was willing to meet head-on, but he also realized that he'd have to navigate it carefully. Unethical competitors like Karen were dangerous, but they also often overreached and got caught in their own webs of deceit.

John started working diligently on his conceptual proposal for Green Revolution, ensuring that it was not just competitively priced but also thoroughly researched and tailored to Kevin's specific needs. He rechecked every clause, recalibrated every projection, and consulted with senior underwriters to make sure he was offering the best possible package.

As the days rolled by, John felt the weight of the challenge he was up against. Yet, at the same time, he felt more alive than he had in months. Each day was a new test, each client meeting a new opportunity to grow and learn. His conversations with Mark and Robert became more detailed, they often helped him to dissect specific negotiations or client challenges, and each time John came away with valuable insights. Kathy kept her encouraging but pragmatic approach, reminding John that the industry was a battlefield where only the best survived. It was a mixed bag of experiences, a mélange of trials, allies, and enemies, but John wouldn't have had it any other way.

He was pushing his own boundaries, laying the groundwork for a long, rewarding career, and perhaps most importantly, learning the fine art of resilience. The upcoming proposal presentation to Kevin loomed large, but John felt ready. After all, his journey had taught him that the most difficult challenges often yield the most satisfying victories. And win or lose, he knew he was already richer for the experience.

As John prepared for another week, his mind circled back to the chapter on reputation. He would not only work to uphold his own but would also strive to elevate the reputation of his agency and the industry at large. Amidst all these challenges and competitions, that was the one thing he could control fully: the quality of his work, the integrity of his actions, and the reputation he was slowly but steadfastly building. Karen, Kathy, Kevin—they were all characters in this unfolding story of his life, but it was up to him to determine what kind of protagonist he would be.

The Ultimate Advantage

John was starting to see the merit of the book's teachings in action, particularly the chapter that emphasized building "Centers of Influence" or COIs. These were the key nodes in any network—the people who could connect you to new opportunities or offer insights and advice. Such centers could be lawyers, accountants, venture capitalists, or other professionals whose work intersected with your own in some way. And so, riding on the peak of his recent, albeit small, successes, John made a plan to connect with people who could really help his career take off.

He began attending industry-specific events, joining webinars, and participating in forums that were hotspots for tech and green energy professionals. It was at these gatherings that he crossed paths with individuals who would soon become invaluable parts of his professional network. At a recent tech conference, for instance, he met Alan, a lawyer specializing in intellectual property rights for tech startups. After a few conversations and a couple of coffee meetings later, they found opportunities to refer clients to each other. Similarly, at a green energy symposium, he met Christine, an accountant who had a long history of working with companies in that sector. Both recognized the value each brought to the table and agreed to keep an eye out for opportunities to share with each other.

Beyond the niche-specific spaces, John also got involved with his local Chamber of Commerce and participated in the Economic Development Program. These platforms gave him access to a broader range of professionals and resources. Among them was Rafael, a seasoned investor, always on the lookout for promising green startups. Not only did Rafael refer a couple of potential clients to John, but he also became an invaluable mentor, offering insights into the business dynamics of new ventures in the green energy sector.

But John didn't just stop at making these connections; he nurtured them. He made it a point to catch up with his COIs regularly, update them on his progress, and discuss trends and challenges in the industry. And the relationships were not just transactional; genuine friendships started to form. Alan, Christine, Rafael, and others were becoming not just professional connections but also personal allies.

During this proactive networking, John was still juggling meetings with new prospects. Thanks to his newly expanded network, these meetings were increasingly coming from warm leads, making the selling process smoother and more enjoyable. Cold calling, a task he had once dreaded, had evolved into an engaging and rewarding activity. His phone calls were no longer shots in the dark; they were calculated moves, supported by a network of individuals who could vouch for his credibility and expertise.

As days turned into weeks, John noticed a profound shift in his perception of his work. It didn't feel like a grind anymore; it felt like he was in his element. The daunting challenges that once kept him up at night now felt like exciting problems to solve. The people he interacted with were no longer just names in a database but vital connections that enriched his professional journey and, in many cases, his personal life as well.

Each day was a learning experience. Alan taught him the intricacies of intellectual property law and how it applied to tech companies. Christine helped him understand the accounting challenges that green energy companies faced, and Rafael provided an investor's perspective on the green energy sector. This informal education, based on years of expertise in the field, gave him nuanced insights into his clients' challenges, enabling him to offer them better, more informed solutions.

Even beyond the realm of insurance, John found himself in deep conversations about sustainability, technology, innovation, and social responsibility. The richness of these discussions often left him amazed at how much there was to know and how interconnected it all was. It was like he had stumbled into a vast, interconnected cave full of valuable gems; all he had to do was explore.

In retrospect, John realized that his job had become a thrilling expedition. He was a spelunker in a sprawling cavern, where each chamber was an industry, each gem a connection, and each inscription on the wall a lesson that led to further growth. And as he ventured deeper into this innermost cave, the luminescence of the gems around him only seemed to get brighter, promising greater treasures ahead.

It wasn't just about selling insurance anymore; it was about being part of something much larger. The apprehension and monotony that once plagued his days were replaced by a newfound enthusiasm and a voracious appetite for knowledge.

I'm not just building a career; I'm crafting a life, John thought, and the realization was as empowering as it was comforting. The challenges would keep coming, of course, but so would the victories—each one lighting his way as he ventured further into the exhilarating labyrinth of his chosen path.

The Ordeal

It felt as if John had hit a wall. The deal with Green Revolution, the one he had been so hopeful about, had fallen through. They opted for a larger agency claiming to have a "special program" that only they could offer. Deep down, John knew this was likely a sales gimmick. But to call them out would make him seem bitter and resentful, a sore loser.

The disappointment felt like a body blow. It wasn't just the loss of a potentially significant client; it was the dent to his confidence, the erosion of his optimism. For a moment, all the progress he had made, all the networking and all the small victories, seemed meaningless. Was he, he wondered, just setting himself up for a string of such failures? Was he truly cut out for this demanding and competitive industry?

It was at this critical juncture that Mark reached out to him, almost as if sensing his despair. "John, remember the book's lesson on ethics and long-term vision," he advised. "You're building something larger than a single deal or even a single client. It's a long-term relationship you're cultivating, not just with Green Revolution but with the entire industry. Keep putting the client's needs first, and success will follow."

His words were wise but somewhat abstract. Mark was essentially telling him that there were greater battles ahead, bigger opportunities, and that ethical conduct and a focus on customer needs would eventually pay off. Still, the loss stung.

Robert, who had just heard about the fiasco, chuckled and said, "Ah, the 'only I can do this because I have the secret sauce' trick. Classic Karen." He leaned back in his chair, crossing his arms. "Listen, John. In this business, people come and go, but reputations last. If Karen wants to cut corners and make hollow promises, let her. You just focus on delivering the best value you can. Sometimes clients get wooed away by flashy claims, but they're not stupid. Many will see through the gimmicks and return to an advisor who

The Ultimate Advantage

has their best interests at heart. Keep your reputation intact, and you'll see how things come full circle."

The conversations with Mark and Robert were illuminating in their own ways. Mark pushed him to think long-term, to focus on the career he was building rather than just the deals he was making. Robert, on the other hand, offered a more practical, cutthroat insight: the industry was filled with players like Karen, who would leverage their firm's clout and make lofty claims to secure deals. But these tactics, Robert implied, had a shelf life.

Spurred by their counsel, John took a step back to assess his situation. He still had a budding network, a growing expertise in his chosen niches, and a list of prospects who were genuinely interested in what he had to offer. The Green Revolution deal was a setback, but it was also a lesson in the unpredictability of the industry.

Realizing he needed a confidence boost, John decided to refocus on the elements he could control. He revisited his marketing strategies, sharpened his pitch, and engaged in even deeper research into the tech and green energy sectors. Simultaneously, he kept up his networking efforts, setting up informational interviews with experts in related fields to broaden his knowledge. It was painstaking work, but it restored his sense of agency. He felt he was better equipped, more prepared for the trials that would inevitably come his way.

And the trials did come, but so did triumphs. Small wins started to accumulate. A tech startup here, a local restaurant there, and a few smaller green energy firms gave him their business. These victories were revitalizing. Although none were as big as the Green Revolution account, each was a steppingstone, a building block, evidence that he was still in the game. More importantly, he noticed a more rewarding trend; he was starting to get referrals. His networking efforts were beginning to pay off, and his reputation for being a reliable, client-focused advisor was getting around.

John also decided to add another layer to his professionalism. Heeding Mark's advice on continual learning, he finally completed his online CIC (Certified Insurance Counselor) course. It was a grueling program, but the information and insights it provided were invaluable. He felt like a more complete insurance advisor, better able to understand and address his clients' various needs.

Weeks turned into months, and the sting of the lost deal with Green Revolution started to fade. John wasn't yet where he wanted to be, but he was far beyond where he began. His reputation was intact, and his resolve was stronger than ever. With each setback, he found himself a bit more resilient, a tad more insightful, and increasingly convinced that success in this challenging industry was not just about the deals you make, but the kind of professional you become.

Reflecting on the journey, John recognized that the real ordeal was not losing a big client but confronting his own doubts and insecurities. In overcoming that internal struggle, in deciding not to cut corners or compromise on his values, he found a stronger, more resilient version of himself.

Mark was right. It wasn't about a single deal; it was about building something far more lasting. And Robert's words had been prophetic. As he started to get new clients—some of them dissatisfied converts from other agencies—John realized that reputation did indeed have a way of coming full circle.

He had crossed a significant threshold, not just in his career but also in his personal development. His ordeal had been an initiation, a rite of passage that had tested and ultimately fortified his character. And as he looked forward to the challenges and opportunities that awaited him, John knew he was ready, come what may, to face them with integrity, resilience, and a long-term vision.

Months had passed since the ordeal of the lost Green Revolution deal, and it felt like years. During that time, John had witnessed an incredible transformation, not only in his career but in himself. His hard work, integrity, and strategic networking through Centers of Influence (COIs) had finally begun to pay off.

The Meeting and the Victory

John felt a rush of adrenaline as he entered the glass-paneled conference room of VirtuAI, the artificial intelligence startup that had been taking the tech world by storm. He knew that today's presentation could be a game-changer for his career and the agency he represented. As he set up his laptop and reviewed his notes, he couldn't help but think of Mark's teachings and the book's chapter on handling objections.

Martin, the CEO of VirtuAI, welcomed him with a warm smile. "Glad you could make it, John. We're interested in hearing what you have to offer."

John nodded, gathering his poise. "Thank you, Martin. I've prepared a conceptual proposal that I believe aligns perfectly with VirtuAI's specific needs and risks."

The Conceptual Proposal

Understanding the Client's Needs

"As you know, AI is an exciting field, but it's also fraught with unique risks," John began, launching into a discussion of the specific risks involved in AI development, including data breaches, compliance issues, and intellectual property disputes.

Martin interjected, "We already have some of those areas covered. What makes your approach different?"

John was ready for this. "What sets us apart is our holistic approach. We not only offer insurance solutions but also risk management strategies that could prevent some of these risks from becoming liabilities in the first place."

Customized Solutions

John proceeded to present the custom-tailored solutions he had developed. "We can offer specialized coverage that evolves as you do, complete with riders for emerging technologies and a dedicated claims service team knowledgeable in tech."

"Sounds promising, but what's the cost?" Martin asked, his eyes narrowing slightly.

Value Proposition

"This is where we bring in the most value. While the initial cost may be on the higher side, think of it as an investment that pays off through minimized risks and fewer potential legal complications down the line."

Martin looked thoughtful but didn't immediately object, encouraging John to continue.

Asking for the Broker of Record (BOR)

"As you can see, our approach is thorough and tailored to your needs. To move forward, we'd like to ask for a Broker of Record letter, effectively allowing us to represent your interests in the insurance marketplace."

"Switching brokers is a big decision," Martin said cautiously.

"Absolutely," John agreed, "and it's not a decision to take lightly. But based on what I've presented today, I believe we can significantly improve upon what you currently have in place."

It was a tense moment as Martin considered it. Finally, he nodded. "Alright, let's do it."

The Reward

John couldn't contain his exhilaration as he left the VirtuAI building. He had done it; he had clinched the deal through a series of carefully planned moves, preemptive answers, and strategic offers. This was his largest client to date—a monumental win for any insurance producer.

As he started his car, a smile spread across his face. Not only had he scored big with VirtuAI, but he had also won an account currently handled by the same agency where Karen, his industry rival, worked. It felt like a little cherry on top.

Back at the agency, news of John's big win spread like wildfire. The atmosphere was electric, and his colleagues—Kathy, Robert, and even the initially skeptical Anthony—were genuinely pleased for him.

The deal was a strong affirmation of his abilities, his preparedness, and the valuable mentorship he'd received from Mark. It showcased the fact that John was not just another producer; he was someone who understood the unique needs of his clients, someone who could offer them real, tangible value.

And so came "the reward," a phase that symbolized a blend of professional triumph and personal growth. John felt an overwhelming sense of accomplishment, but also a renewed sense of purpose and passion for his work.

This, he thought, was just the beginning.

The victory was transformative. Not only did it reinvigorate his self-belief and ambition, but it also firmly cemented his reputation within the agency and the wider industry. Word started getting around that John was someone who not only closed deals but provided real, substantial value to his clients. This was the tipping point, the watershed moment he had been working towards.

But the reward was not just professional; it was deeply personal. The financial windfall from the deal allowed John to do something he'd dreamed of but never felt secure enough to plan—a vacation to Hawaii with Carmen, his steadfast girlfriend who had been his emotional rock through all the highs and lows.

The vacation was magical from the get-go, but what made it truly unforgettable was a specific day. After an adrenaline-filled morning of diving in the reef, exploring the enchanting underwater world, John had another surprise up his sleeve. He had chartered a private sailboat to take them around the Big Island. As the sun dipped towards the horizon, painting the sky in shades of orange and pink, John knew the moment was right.

He turned to Carmen, his face flushed from the wind and the excitement. "I've been doing a lot of thinking," he said, fumbling in his pocket for the small box he had hidden there. "This past year has been an incredible journey. I've faced challenges and tasted success, but none of it would mean anything without you by my side. I can't imagine a future that doesn't have you in it."

Before his nerves could get the better of him, he got down on one knee and presented the ring. "Carmen, will you marry me?"

Her eyes filled with tears, and she nodded, too choked up to speak. The kiss they shared as he slid the ring onto her

The Ultimate Advantage

finger was the embodiment of all they had been through and all that awaited them—unknown yet promising.

Back home, the rewards continued to pour in. John became the agency's fastest validated producer. His newfound success didn't go unnoticed in the industry either. An invitation to speak at a significant technology summit on the subject of risk management arrived, where he would have the opportunity to address over 300 business owners.

As he prepared for the summit, the significance of the moment struck him. This speaking engagement was not merely a professional milestone; it was a testament to his journey. The invitation to speak was the industry's way of acknowledging that he had something valuable to share, that he had insights born of both failures and triumphs.

In a way, it felt like life had come full circle. He was no longer the nervous, doubting newcomer at a BIG I event, hanging on to every word from seasoned professionals like Mark. He was now the one whose experiences and insights others might find valuable.

As he reflected on these rewards—his largest client, a strengthened reputation, an engagement to the woman he loved, and an emerging position as a thought leader in his industry—John felt both humbled and empowered.

The journey had been fraught with challenges and setbacks, but each struggle had sculpted him, molded him into a better professional and a more resilient person. And for all that he had gained, John knew that the most significant reward was the experience itself—the lessons learned, the resilience and strength of character he had built, and the love deepened.

It was, he realized, only the beginning. And what a promising beginning it was.

The Ultimate Advantage

As the sun set on another successful quarter, John sat in his new, spacious office, pondering the journey that had brought him here. The walls were adorned with framed pictures of his mentors, his team, and memorable events where he had been a keynote speaker. His desk held a stack of industry accolades. Most notably, the corner shelf displayed a glass trophy with an inscription that read, "Top Producer of the Year in Tech and Green Energy" sectors—a category his agency had created just for him.

Giving Back

John's calendar was usually jam-packed with meetings, strategy sessions, and speaking engagements. But despite the hectic schedule, he made it a point to set aside time for something just as important to him—mentoring.

Remembering his early days of struggle, he reached out to the newest recruits at the agency. Once a month, he organized "newbie lunches" to discuss challenges, answer questions, and most importantly, to remind them that every successful person was once where they were now.

"Your beginning doesn't define you," he would say, a phrase he borrowed from Mark, his own mentor. "What defines you is how you navigate the path ahead. It's about showing up every day, being adaptable, and never stopping the pursuit of learning."

Structuring Success

Beyond mentoring, John was also busy building the internal infrastructure of his now-flourishing division. When he started out, he was a one-man army, handling everything from client meetings to executing marketing campaigns. Now he had an entire team—an Account Manager, Lisa, who was brilliant at customer relationship management; and an Account Executive, Tim, a prodigy in identifying potential leads and closing deals.

The Ultimate Advantage

Together, they created a system where each lead went through a meticulously planned journey streamlined with the help of automation, right from the first email to finalizing contracts. The CRM was tweaked to flag potential challenges before they escalated into problems, enabling preemptive action.

"What we have here is a well-oiled machine," Tim would often say, and he was right. The internal processes they had set up were paying dividends. Not only were they acquiring new clients at a steady pace, but client retention rates had also never been higher.

Marking His Territory

One of the highlights of John's career was the industry events he attended as a keynote speaker. He relished the opportunity to speak to rooms full of business owners, fellow producers, and even competitors. Over time, John became a recognizable face and an authoritative voice in both the tech and green energy sectors. It was a far cry from the days when his emails would get no replies and his calls would go unanswered. Now, people were not just listening; they were taking notes.

John often discussed risk management, market trends, and emerging technologies, framing them all within the lens of insurance. "Understanding your risks is the first step to mitigating them," he would say, encapsulating complex ideas in easily digestible phrases. His sessions were among the most attended, and he often had a queue of people waiting to talk to him afterward.

In parallel, he wrote articles, blog posts, and even contributed to a couple of industry white papers. His marketing efforts had transcended from mere lead generation to thought leadership.

The Sweet Smell of Success

As his reputation grew, so did his portfolio. From small startups to giant corporations, John had a diverse range of clients, but what gave him the most satisfaction was his specialization in the tech and green energy sectors. These were not just industries for him; they were a passion.

John wasn't just surviving; he was thriving. And it wasn't just about the money or the status. It was about the fulfillment he felt every day, the joy he found in mentoring someone, the thrill he got in cracking a tough client, and the peace he found in knowing he was exactly where he wanted to be.

Yet, he knew this wasn't the end. It was a beautiful chapter in an ongoing story. He still had more to achieve, more to give back, and more to learn. As he looked at his life, both professional and personal—he was married now, to Carmen, his pillar of support—he felt grateful.

Grateful to his mentors, to his team, and to every single experience that shaped him, good or bad. But most of all, grateful to himself for having the courage to keep going during those early, tough days, for taking that first, shaky step on a road that led him back to a place of triumph, and for realizing that the road doesn't end; it just unfolds into new beginnings.

Five years had flown by since John embarked on his journey in the insurance industry, and they had been years of progress and triumph. However, life has a way of delivering humbling moments just when you start to feel invincible. His biggest green energy client, a company led by Coline, was considering switching their insurance coverage to a more established competitor. Ironically, the competitor was none other than Karen.

Preparing for Battle

Remembering the wisdom of the book that had become his bible, John was ready to be a hero for his client. He had consistently educated his clients about market trends and benchmarked their performance against their peers, which gave him hope that Coline would not fall for the "exclusive program" allure that Karen often touted.

A curveball came his way—both agencies were to present their proposals to the client at the same meeting. Karen would go first, followed by John, as the incumbent agent. John knew he had to make the most compelling case for his client's needs and show them the value he could bring to the table.

Karen's Presentation

Karen entered the meeting room in a pantsuit, her short hair impeccably styled, a stark contrast to the laid-back persona she usually displayed at industry gatherings. She arrived in a Prius, conspicuously eco-conscious, especially compared to her gas-guzzling Mustang she'd show off at Big I Meetings.

With a team of four people flanking her, Karen began her presentation, leaning heavily into her agency's credentials. "We are the largest agency writing green energy companies in the country, extending our services even internationally," she boasted. She further talked about her unique access to special carriers and concluded how her large agency could offer security and market leverage.

John's Turn

Karen's presentation was a hard act to follow, but John was ready. Dressed in a modest but elegant suit, he stood up, his team of two at his side. He opened his presentation by directly addressing the client's needs and questions. "What we offer is a partnership, not just an insurance policy. We're not just brokers; we're your advocates," he began.

John went on to detail the customized solutions he'd been implementing over the years, which were aligned with the client's long-term goals and industry benchmarks. "Moreover," he added, "we've consistently been ahead of the curve in identifying risks specific to the green energy sector and devising strategies to mitigate them."

The tension was palpable, and the stakes were high. Then Coline, the client, threw in another question: "How would you both feel about assigning markets?"

The Final Confrontation

John had anticipated this. After a chat with Robert, he had suggested to Coline that if she felt the larger agency could offer more, they could each pick the markets they wanted to present to. Karen could bring her "special markets," while John would work the renewal as he usually would. They agreed to meet back in six weeks.

Six weeks later, they gathered again. Karen presented first, offering numbers, facts, and figures. Her proposal was thorough, but it was also complex and somewhat generic. John's presentation focused on the client. He spoke about continued partnership and their innovation in risk management, showcasing how he had helped the client reduce their TCOR and avoid risks in the past.

"Both presentations are compelling," Coline began, "but we've decided to continue our journey with John." It was the ultimate validation of his dedication to value-driven service. Even Karen had to give him a forced nod, conceding defeat.

As John walked out of the meeting room, the weight of the moment sank in. He had not only retained his biggest client but had also outclassed Karen, the epitome of a tough competitor. He felt reborn, energized, and reminded of why he had entered this business in the first place.

The Ultimate Advantage

The victory was sweet, but the journey was far from over. That evening, he found himself opening the well-worn pages of that old book again, realizing that even heroes need to revisit their origin stories to appreciate how far they've come and to gather the strength for the challenges that lie ahead.

He also realized that this victory wasn't just his own; it was a collective win for his mentors, his team, and even his clients who trusted him. Most of all, it was a testament to the resilience, hard work, and ethical commitment he had adhered to throughout his career. And so, as he closed that book, he knew that the next chapter in his professional life was waiting to be written, and he couldn't wait to pen it down.

Conclusion

As we approach the final pages of *The Ultimate Advantage*, it is crucial to reflect on the journey we've embarked upon together. The world of commercial insurance sales is nothing short of demanding. It's a dynamic dance of evolving strategies, a continuous drive to be more, to know more. In this book, you've acquired battle-hardened techniques to not only navigate this intricate world but to truly stand out and dominate.

I extend my heartfelt gratitude for allowing me the privilege of accompanying you on this path of growth. Investing in this guide signifies your dedication to excellence, a trait that already sets you apart. My hope is that the teachings within these pages remain a beacon, guiding you through challenges and illuminating your successes.

Now, as we close this chapter, the journey doesn't end here. We've curated an accompanying sales journal tailored to complement *The Ultimate Advantage*. This journal is designed to be your day-to-day companion, capturing reflections, insights, and tracking your progress as you apply the strategies detailed in this guide. I sincerely hope you seek out this invaluable resource, enhancing your trajectory in the competitive landscape of commercial insurance.

In *The Ultimate Advantage*, we delved deep into the psyche of successful sales professionals, understanding that it isn't about the number of policies sold but the relationships cultivated and nurtured. Remember, in this field, your reputation, integrity, and ability to genuinely connect with clients will always be your most potent tools.

Stay driven. In times of doubt or challenge, recall the strategies and philosophies discussed in this guide. Let them be the foundation upon which you build your empire, brick by brick, policy by policy. The commercial insurance realm is vast and, at times, unforgiving, but with the tools you now possess, it is yours to master.

To all the agents, whether budding or seasoned, let *The Ultimate Advantage* "" serve as a constant reminder that success is a journey, not a destination. Every client

The Ultimate Advantage

interaction, every policy written, and every hurdle overcome is a step closer to your ultimate goal of becoming the pinnacle of success in commercial insurance sales. Keep learning, keep growing, and remember: in this ever-competitive world, you now have the ultimate advantage.

Thank you for choosing *The Ultimate Advantage*. It's been an honor to share my experiences and insights with you. Here's to your unparalleled success in the commercial insurance world and to the many accomplishments that await you on the horizon.